ROCK

WATER

WILD

ROCK

WATER

WILD

AN ALASKAN LIFE

Nancy Lord

UNIVERSITY OF NEBRASKA PRESS
LINCOLN AND LONDON

Acknowledgments for the use of previously published
material appear on page xiv, which constitutes an
extension of the copyright page.

∞

Library of Congress Cataloging-in-Publication Data

Lord, Nancy.
Rock, water, wild : an Alaskan life / Nancy Lord.
p.   cm.
ISBN 978-0-8032-2515-2 (cloth : alk. paper)
1. Lord, Nancy. 2. Alaska — Biography. 3. Alaska —
Description and travel. 4. Lord, Nancy — Travel —
Alaska. 5. Outdoor life — Alaska. 6. Country
life — Alaska. 7. Natural history — Alaska. 8. Alaska —
Environmental conditions. 9. Nature — Effect of human
beings on — Alaska. 10. Human ecology — Alaska.
I. Title.
F910.7.L67A3 2009
979.8′051—dc22
2009004335

Set in Garamond Premier Pro by Bob Reitz.
Designed by Nathan Putens.

For those who follow, that they

might still breathe mountain air,

catch fish, and know bears

CONTENTS

I was seven years old and living in New Hampshire when Alaska became a state. My family lived on the same city street that my mother's parents and grandparents had lived on, which is to say that my people had always stuck close to home. It was a very long trip that took us all the way across Vermont to visit my father's family on the far side of Lake Champlain. Alaska, certainly, did not exist on our maps. The year 1959, though, must have brought the new state to the pages of newspapers and magazines. I learned about a land full of mountains and polar bears, Eskimo people who drove dogsleds and fished through ice, an almost-unimaginable beauty.

That year or the next my Brownie troop put on a patriotic play, featuring the new pair of states — Alaska and Hawaii. In my memory, I got to play the part of Alaska, although I'm not sure that my memory can be trusted on this. I certainly remember a fur coat being involved, opposite Hawaii's grass skirt and lei. I coveted both the wearing of the coat and the wondrous idea of a far and frozen land that, however foreign, was *ours*.

In fourth grade we were allowed to choose any of the fifty states for a project, and of course I chose Alaska. I filled my report with pictures cut from *National Geographic* — bears, and caribou, and log cabins breathing columns of smoke. I wrote "chapters" gathered from the encyclopedia, about Alaska's geography, history, and economy, and I colored a map to show the terrain and locations of "products" like metals and fish. My cover featured the eight-stars-of-gold-on-a-field-of-blue Alaska flag designed by the Aleut boy Benny Benson when he was thirteen years old.

A couple of years later I found Peter Freuchen's *Book of the Eskimos* on my parents' bookshelf and devoured the descriptions of the far north and its inhabitants — Greenland being close enough to Alaska, in this case. Later still, I spent my pocket money on newsstand copies of *The Alaska Sportsman*, with its articles about bush pilots and frozen mammoths and, in the back, advertisements for government homesteads.

I first reached Alaska when I was nineteen, and I made the permanent move with my partner two years later. Ken and I negotiated location — he wanted to be a commercial fisherman — and chose a coastal town.

I never worried about what I would do in Alaska. From the beginning, I understood that my life depended on *place*, as opposed to traditional concerns like job opportunities and family ties. In the right place, my life would find its shape, as indeed it did. I worked at whatever jobs allowed me to be where I wanted to be — a strategy that turned out to be perfect for a writer, allowing me a variety of experiences, from recording the weather to selling cross-country skis and developing state energy policy, all within a seasonal, flexible schedule. Ken and I spent many happy summers commercial fishing for salmon. I learned to pay attention, the most essential writer's work. If I never entered into the high adventures I might have dreamed about as a child, I did in fact become a kind of explorer. As a writer I could go anywhere to learn everything I could about whatever interested me. I could probe that ever-fascinating "human condition." The act of writing was all about trying to figure out what I thought about what I'd learned and why what I thought had any importance. In Alaska I didn't set out to be a writer but became one along the way.

This book is a collection of writings, mostly from the last decade, that, taken together, present my life along its path of determining who I would be and what I would care about. I've been fortunate not only to have lived a rich life in a small town locally touted as "cosmic" and at our summer fish camp but to have traveled both within and outside of Alaska, and the essays reflect my exploration into all those places and what I found in them. I hasten to add that the book is neither *about* Alaska nor *about* me; it's not any kind of travelogue, and I'm not that interesting as a person. The chapters are *essays* in the original meaning of the word — that is, *attempts* to learn, to discover, to wander around in ideas as I try to reach some understandings. They proceed from some considerations of the young person I was, to adventures and inquiries in Alaska, to more distant lands. Some common themes prevail: I'm interested in thinking, perhaps above all, about relationships — among science, history, traditional teachings, politics, art — and in the interconnectedness of all things. I'm fond of the natural world and what we can learn from it and from those who have lived closely with it, and I believe that we ought to talk about our responsibilities to our one world and all who share it.

I have written largely of Alaska, in this book and others, not only because Alaska is my home and thus the place I know best but because it's the last place in America that's big enough and wild enough to hold the intact landscapes and the dreams that are so absent today from almost everywhere else. Alaska offers us both remarkable beauty and examples of the visible linkages between natural systems, history, and the present. Alaska is home to people with ancient ways of knowing what it means to live respectfully with the natural world. It's my hope that this book will encourage readers to search their own home places for some of that same beauty and connectedness, and understanding. I hope that they might protect and even restore what they love.

ACKNOWLEDGMENTS

This work encompasses many years of my writing life — indeed goes all the way back to my beginnings as a writer, before I even knew I might become one. I thus owe an enormous debt to those who, along the way, contributed to my education in the broadest sense and allowed or helped me to find my place in the world. Some of those people appear, by name or otherwise, in this book; others are equally appreciated.

My parents, of course, were foremost in introducing me to the natural world and allowing me to indulge my passions for reading, writing, and living in Alaska. My partner Ken Castner has both shared my life and supported my quests for understanding and the right words. I am forever grateful to those I think of as my writing community — beginning with Homer friends who met to share potluck salmon and stories, to fellow grad students at Vermont College and fellow "fellows" at artist colonies and residency programs and, increasing, to the growing number of my Alaska peers who write so well and share so generously. I also thank Carol Swartz for enthusiastically fostering the literary arts in our town, the many editors who have encouraged and published my work over the years, and the public libraries that provide me and every American with free access to books and research materials.

For their very helpful influence on the work in this book, I'd particularly like to thank Jack Coogan, David Roberts, Sue Silverman, Tom Kizzia, Amy Friedman, Peggy Shumaker, Marybeth Holleman, Peter Thomson, Paul Rauber, and Ron Spatz.

I'm very grateful for my long-term relationship with agent Elizabeth Wales and for the fresh eye and vision of editor Ladette Randolph.

Much of this work was undertaken at artist colonies or residency programs. I wish to thank the benefactors, staff, and fellow residents at Ucross Foundation, Ragdale Foundation, Fundacion Valparaiso, Djerassi Foundation, Writers' Colony at Dairy Hollow, and Blue Mountain Center.

The Alaska State Council on the Arts and the Rasmuson Foundation both provided fellowship support for the writing of this book and associated travel, and I am enormously thankful for that.

※

Individual essays in this book originally appeared, often in different form and sometimes with different titles, in the following publications:

"On Rereading *Siddhartha*," "Enough," and "The Farthest Island,"
    Alaska Quarterly Review
"In the Giant's Hand," *Travelers' Tales Alaska*
"Report from the Rookeries," "Words Honor Place," and "From an
    Old World Sea," *Sierra*
"Zen Moose," *The New York Times*
"Honk," *OnEarth*
"Quiet Time," *Alaska Magazine*
"The Hidden Half," "A Border Runs Through It," and "Hope is the
    Thing in Spring," *Anchorage Daily News*
"How to Bear Witness" and "I Met a Man Who Has Seen the Ivory-
    billed Woodpecker, and This is What He Told Me," *Fourth
    Genre*
"Magadan Luck," *Uncommon Waters: Women Write About Fishing*
    (Seal Press: Seattle, 1991)
"The Rings," *Interdisciplinary Studies in Literature and the
    Environment*
"A Bigger World," *America West*
"The Experiment," *Crosscurrents North: Alaskans on the Environment*
"Being Peter," *Under the Sun*.

ROCK

WATER

WILD

ON THE WAY

There is always one moment

in childhood when the door

opens and the future is let in.

GRAHAM GREENE,

THE POWER AND THE GLORY

BEING PETER

In John McPhee's 1977 classic, *Coming Into the Country*, he describes a typical Alaskan yard full of tarps, tires, oil drums, and dismantled snow machines, and comments that "when you drive along an old back road in the Lower Forty-Eight and come across a yard full of manufactured debris. . . you have come upon a fragment of Alaska. The people inside are Alaskans who have not yet left for the north." He's not mean-spirited in this; he makes an honest and reasonably accurate observation about what it takes to live in the north.

I long ago absorbed McPhee's remark into my own psyche, and in my travels I occasionally meet people whom I think of as "Alaskans who just haven't left yet." I mean that positively, and I mean that I recognize a kinship — perhaps in someone who's never even *thought* of Alaska. That person has a certain restlessness of spirit, a comfort in space and quiet, and more than a streak of independence. He or she is capable of self-invention, or reinvention.

Alaskans — those of us who came here from somewhere else — tell similar stories: *I came over the hill* (or to the beach, or into the forest) *and knew I was home.*

And so it's clear to me that I was an Alaskan long before I knew I would make the physical move. I was a child with imagination, a sense of adventure, and a longing for something indefinably *more*. I would live in woods and by a lagoon, and I would fly. I don't mean airplanes. I mean *really fly*.

I became a sort of prototype of a future Alaskan.

I was Peter Pan.

❧

I don't recall when or how the book came to me. I do remember that it had a jacketless green cloth cover, and I suppose it must have been a hand-me-down from my sister or brother once I'd gotten past the pious lessons of Dick-and-Jane schoolbooks. There might have been some illustrated plates tucked inside, but they're not what I remember. What I remember is reading word after word after word, and that the words made pictures and the pictures a world. And what a world it was! Children in their nightclothes flying past the stars, hollow trees dropping into an underground house, lagoons and pirate ships, stealthy Indians, fairies, a ticking crocodile, Peter Pan and his devoted boys. Words — mere words — could do all that. Well, words and *me*. Wasn't I taking those words into my brain and making from them something that was mine? Wasn't *I* the one inhabiting that magical land, having those outrageous adventures?

The unassuming cover, when the book lay closed beside me, had only its title and, beneath it, "J. M. Barrie." Who *was* this person? I had not, perhaps, thought much before about books being the creations of people. Books were books, objects that existed unto themselves. Had some one person actually written down this story and, if so, where had the story come from?

There was, of course, the televised version, the musical starring Mary Martin. My family didn't own a television when it was first broadcast, in 1955, but in subsequent years I counted myself among the millions of American children who awaited its annual appearance, who clapped mightily for Tinker Bell's recovery, who sang along with the songs. Each year I strove to learn more of the lyrics, but other than that, the movie seemed a tepid substitute for the book and for the stretches of my own imagination. Mary Martin was not my idea of Peter. She was so obviously a grown woman, with bound breasts inside her leafy boy costume, and the wired harness that sailed her across the stage was, well, *stupid*.

❧

"Boy, why are you crying?"

I hear my child's voice, exactly how I coached Wendy to ask me, Peter, this early line from the book, and how Wendy — my friend, Phyllis, the sweetest, most Wendyish girl I knew — would repeat it back to me. And we would be off, with Judy and Paula and Lynn and whatever other members of the Peter Pan Club I had assembled in a New Hampshire backyard, to act out again the story of the fly-away children, the swearing fairy, and the rest. I pantomime rubbing my shadow with soap, Wendy tells me I'm ignorant and takes up her sewing, Tinker Bell flits and shouts "you silly ass," and then I crow like a rooster, and we all crow and say "ass" and spread fairy dust around and run and leap and hold out our arms like wings.

"I'm flying!"

"I'm flying!"

"I'm flying!"

We're light on our feet and dancing in the air, and the feel of all that lightness and energy is almost exactly like soaring toward the stars, "straight on 'til morning." Almost exactly, if you believe.

Lines from the book, or the movie, or my own acting out and teaching of the sacred text swarm back to me still, carrying with them every bit of sweet resonance from that world. I hear the crowing in my mind and feel that satisfying catch at the bottom of my throat as the *ur-ur-ur-urrrrr* tumbles out. I'm drawn back to all the defiance in the song I led us through again and again:

> I won't grow up! I won't grow up!
> I don't want to go to school. I don't want to go to school.
> Just to learn to be a parrot. Just to learn to be a parrot.
> And recite a silly rule. And recite a silly rule.
> 'Cause growing up means it would be
> Beneath my dignity to climb a tree.
> I'll never grow up, never grow up, never grow a-up, not me!
> Not I!
> Not me!!

For the longest time I thought the word in the third line was *parent*. Parent/parrot. The distinction wasn't all that crucial.

❦

I was Peter because I had invented the Peter Pan Club and was its president. I suppose I selected all the members, although I don't remember there being any exclusivity, other than the disallowance of *boys*. We were an all-girls' club, and any girls who would have me as their leader could find a home in my pageant of lost boys and other free spirits. I assigned roles, and I found in my Michael, my John, my Tootles and Twins sufficient character to undertake the necessary and assorted conditions of servitude, silliness, and learning of lines.

"A little less noise there!"

"You silly ass!"

"Tut tut!"

"I complain of Nibs!"

"What would Peter do?" Peter, of course, would look between his legs at the slavering wolves, and they would all run away.

I don't, in fact, recall our play as a collaborative venture. I was the keeper of the text and the vision, as much a dictator as any Peter ever was. Today, I'm embarrassed to say, I recall the *parts* better than most of the *girls*. The girls may have been my friends, my classmates and my companions in scouts and at Sunday School, but when we entered Neverland they were actors on the stage. The actual girls came and went; they switched roles as necessary and convenient. But Tootles was always Tootles, and Tinker Bell, Tinker Bell.

We certainly recognized that we were girls in a boys' story, but that was neither obstacle nor expressive of gender-identity confusion. We all knew that boys had more fun. Boys got to wear comfortable clothes and play sports. They got to ride bikes wherever they wanted and to disappear into woods for unexplained hours. Boy Scouts went camping and learned to tie knots. Girls were supposed to play quietly, preferably indoors, and cooperatively, as in rope jumping. Girl Scouts sewed aprons and sold cookies. For field trips our troop dutifully entertained old people and disabled children with patriotic songs.

As Peter I had not only the best part in the story but the best role I could think of, among all the stories I knew. Peter could fly *and* fight pirates. Peter took care of others (more spectacularly than Wendy, playing at being a mother). Peter was utterly adventurous, and he crowed like a crazy rooster. Storybook girls — even the ones with "pluck" — were too much in the real world for me, too serious, too likely to pursue moral rectitude. Nancy Drew in her little roadster was nowhere near my type. Peter was, quite simply, the self-contained, self-assured, freedom-loving escapee I would be.

And the name — I liked *Peter*. I liked the sharpness of the two consonant sounds, the cleanness of the whole. In the back of the dictionary, it was a name with a meaning — a solid Greek identity: *rock*. I had never cared for my own name — the nagging Ns, the soft and babyish C, the no-meaning except it was a little Ann and Ann had something to do with grace. *Nancy* didn't feel like me. *Peter* did. The club members called me Peter, and if anyone else wondered or looked askance, that didn't trouble me. When I heard *Peter*, I felt like I was someone, someone so much more solid than any Nancy could ever be.

If Peter's was a boys' story, it transformed under my command. Peter could fight pirates, but the gory business of swashbuckling and stabbing was not all that appealing, and I was repulsed by the idea that Peter — I — would have cut off poor Hook's arm. Plot elements, in fact, were much less interesting to me than what I would now call a more organic way of imagining life in Neverland. As our pack flew and fluttered, I was always careful to emphasize the physical points of the island we inhabited. We embraced the forest and slid through its hollow trees, coming and going from our secret hiding places. In long twining lines, and stopping to set our ears to the ground, we followed the paths of Indians and wolves. We sailed upon the fabulous lagoon, surrounded by jungle plants, birds in floating nests, and tail-kicking mermaids. There was that crocodile, too, but it always safely ticked.

As a club we practiced our flying techniques and put domestic order to our underground quarters. We concerned ourselves, like the women we pretended we would not become, with relationships. Wendy, cooking and sewing, cared for Peter and all the boys, and the rest of us acted at being annoyed with one another, letting loose small cruelties we might not have allowed ourselves in our real lives. We might tell the girl who was Tootles that she was eating too many cookies, but since we were telling Tootles and not the girl, and because our characters were known to be impolite, we could be as rude as we liked. *Tootles, you fat slob, don't eat all the cookies.* And of course, since I was president and captain, I could be just as bossy and demanding as I liked. I was Peter!

We could, however, also be solicitous. We gave flying lessons and encouragement to John and Michael while tossing fistfuls of fairy dust; told stories to the poor, ignorant, pram-fallen boys; released Tinker Bell each time she got locked in a drawer. We liked to get Twin and Twin confused. We followed Tiger Lily on soft little cat feet, and then we war-whooped and beat on drums. We sang, and the point was to sing like a bunch of lost boys who'd never had to face piano lessons or choir practice — badly and with as much volume and joy as possible.

Neverland nights were lit by balls of light that were fairies, and the air was filled with the sounds of little bells. These were not girly-girl ideas of fairies — prissy points of light and sweetness — but fairies with personality. "A quite common girl," Peter explains Tinker Bell to Wendy, as if to excuse the fairy's fits of temper and to diminish her magic. Her job in the fairy world, after all, was as a tinker — to mend pots and kettles for the other fairies. If the British, class-minded use of "common" escaped me, I at least got the joke — the counter to tinkling and twinkling and all the ordinary fairy orthodoxy. And Tinker Bell swore! When had we ever met such a fairy? We felt wild and reckless even as we were authorized — by a book. We twittered with Tinker Bell, as often as possible: "You silly ass!"

I don't think I ever understood that J. M. Barrie was British and that his Peter Pan emerged from another time and culture. I only thought that he had to be a really smart person to have thought of all he had and to have invented such beautiful language, too. Captain Hook was "cadaverous" and "blackavised," his "miscreants" "begirt with weapons." Peter and the boys lived among the pampas, with coracles, sometimes in pandemonium and always with "ecstasies innumerable." "Tut, tut" became my — and our — favorite commentary, applied with vigorous indiscrimination. You were late for school? Tut, tut! You had another peanut butter and jelly sandwich? Tut, tut! You need to go home now? Tut, tut, Tootles!

I shouldn't forget the pirates. Although pirates did not belong to the club and I had taken on Wendy's antiviolence position, we did sometimes engage with pirates, a.k.a. actual boys. On the school playground, if we didn't wage mock battles, we did identify who the pirates were, and we did chase them back and forth across the territory, or — turning — let them chase us. We captured them, or they captured us, and then we shouted about the crocodile and, superior to pirates in every way, we flew off crowing.

I can only remember one pirate in particular — the one I appointed Captain Hook. He was a nice boy by the name of Bradley, and I secretly liked him. The reason I thought he made a good Hook was that, in lieu of a hooked arm, he wore a brace on his leg. He had a thick shoe and the metal brace that stiffened his leg, and so he ran with a kind of lurch that seemed perfect for someone we would taunt as Hook. It did not occur to me at the time that singling out Bradley for his physical condition might have been unkind.

❧

"A little less noise there!" we mocked the absent Mr. Darling.

The lack of adults in Peter's world was precisely the main attraction. Peter, who ran away the day he was born, had done just fine without grown-ups telling him what to do. (As the song went, "Growing up is awfuller than all the awful things that ever were.") Our Neverland, we knew, could not be imagined, much less entered, by anyone beyond the club. That was very much the point.

I remained in awe of J. M. Barrie. How could he — an adult — have so perfectly understood children? He knew we should be allowed to conspire among ourselves against the adult and proper world. He was our coconspirator.

And so the Peter Pan Club carried on in the margins of our otherwise organized world of school and scouts and family dinners. We didn't advertise it to the adults in our lives, and those adults — if they overheard us bellowing out silly show tunes — didn't impose on us. This was, of course, still a time when children were allowed to form their own alliances and invent their own play, as opposed to being scheduled for theater camps and matched-jersey sports teams. If I was too bossy, no adult withered me with a word or a sharp look. If we were reckless with one another's feelings or physical well-being, no one interceded; we dealt with the consequences ourselves. Children were — the story said so — gay and innocent and *heartless*.

Parents could not understand *Peter Pan*, I thought, and that was all right; they weren't meant to. Parents approved of pretty books, like the illustrated ones by Tasha Tudor my mother pressed upon me. *My Grandmother's Doll* was all pastel sweetness, with no Indians, lagoons, or secret underground dwellings. Parents also liked instructive books: the little engine that could if it kept trying, the little red hen that worked hard and got to eat her cake. There was no moral ambiguity in those texts, and nothing to send sparks streaking across the sky.

❧

As inferior as I knew the televised play version to be, I always looked forward to its once-a-year appearance. Aside from the chance to learn more song lyrics, I especially liked the part where Tinker Bell drank the poison meant for Peter and had to be saved.

Quick! Quick! Her light's getting dimmer. If you believe in fairies, clap your hands!

Of course I clapped. Not because I believed in fairies, but because I believed in theater.

In general, I was not a believer. As the youngest child in my family, I'd never even had a chance with Santa Claus or the Easter Bunny, and the idea of a God in the sky had always seemed to me equally improbable.

I couldn't believe in Peter Pan's magic, either, in the most literal sense. I did not, for example, leap off my bedpost or roof as some other Peter-enchanted children apparently did. (Much later I would read that fairy dust was added to the original play after too many children broke bones and knocked out teeth.) I'm sure I knew from the beginning that, really, there was no physical place resembling Neverland beyond the stars; there were no fairies, no children who could fly, not even any big dogs that could be trusted as nursemaids.

But, in another important sense, I *did* believe. I understood that *Peter Pan* was really about belief and the power of make-believe. A make-believe world could be real because it could make you want to believe it was, because you could will it into being so, at least in your mind. The imagination was a real place where a person could go, and the life found there could be richly detailed and as complete and satisfying as its possessor could wish. The important distinction was not between what was real and what was not but between the outer world and the inner one. When I was Peter I could create for myself a state of being that was as real to me as I wanted it to be. When I flew, I went to the space that connected J. M. Barrie's words with my own imagination — right where I wanted to be.

Fussing over Tinker Bell, sprinkling fairy dust, running so lightly I convinced myself I was flying, the places I went in my nighttime dreams and my wandering daydreams — these were not about actual belief. They were about the suspension of disbelief, about letting myself think *what if*. What if there was a land I could design just as I wished, what if I could fly, what if I was in charge of my own life? And then? And then? What if I found a home there, in that inner, knowing, creating, exploring place?

Clap your hands!

I imagined a deafening noise across the land. All good children and their encouraging parents would save Tinker Bell, but there was something equally entrancing about that theater. In the murky depths of my consciousness, I began to understand something about *power*. If all those people believed in one thing, or pretended to, or wanted to, they could be a force in the world. Who could organize people like that? Peter could do that. Or Mary Martin acting as Peter. Or maybe not. Maybe all the Peters in the world were only creations, and maybe the real power to convince and command lay with the mysterious J. M. Barrie. It was *writers* who created worlds (fabulous, fanciful, true) and then invited in the rest of us — all those thousands and millions and billions as I imagined the clapping believers to be.

※

I don't remember an end to the Peter Pan Club. I think it was as late as sixth grade when I was still organizing our members on the playground to chase Hook and the other pirates to the other end of the playground, and I remember a teacher sending me back to the "girls' side" with instructions to leave the boys alone. Even then, our attentions to the pirates had gotten adolescently complicated; the chase had changed to somehow wanting to be captured by the pirates and to find out who liked whom.

I suppose the girls simply fell away, just as they abandoned scouting. There were other things to do: ballroom dancing lessons, hanging around horse stables, playing Beatles records and arguing whether Paul or George was cuter. Day by day our lives were getting fuller and more complicated, more as we might shape them to our wills. I understood the childishness of a club pledged to "never growing up."

Life imitated art. The book finally fizzled to an end, and it was not an ending that ever gave me any satisfaction. Sad parents and earthly lives, it seemed, beckoned. Wendy and her brothers flapped back to their nursery, taking all the lost boys with them. Only Peter stayed in Neverland, living in treetops with fairies, the same forever. If Wendy was released from her responsible life to visit Peter, it was only to clean his house. As she grew to be a woman the space between their worlds grew harder and harder to navigate.

❧

The passage of years has not been kind to *Peter Pan*. In today's cultural atmosphere, of course, the story is a universe away from political correctness. The scary pirates are swarthy and black, and poor disabled Hook's metal arm is a symbol of absolute evil. The Indians, described as belonging to the "Piccaninny" tribe, collect scalps and refer to Peter as the "Great White Father."

Adults now, we may shake our heads and want to spare our children the prejudicial depictions of blacks, Indians, wolves, people with artificial limbs, and Wendy as a housecleaner. We may shiver and turn away from the story's cutthroat violence. Sure, these elements can be, and have been, altered and downplayed in modern tellings and productions, but the results have been the kind of thin gruel Peter would have overturned in its pot.

Once, when visiting my brother's family, I was delighted to find *Peter Pan* on my niece's bookshelf, and she and I snuggled down to read it before bed. But it was not *Peter Pan*. It was a bastardized substitute with cartoony figures, and the text was the baldest kind of superficial plotting. Tinker Bell wasn't naughty. Nobody said things like, "Brimstone and gall, what cozening is here?" The lost boys didn't dance around wildly and throw pillows. My niece fidgeted with the bed covers, and I tried to ad lib some of the story as I knew it, but the illustrations were so wrong—Peter as an elf-eared leprechaun with slippers like pea pods!—that it was like trying to match apples to orangutans. If I'd been the person I wanted to be, I'd have closed the book and found the words for a land where my niece and I might have adventured together. But I'd lived too much in the real, adult world, and I couldn't find my way. I flipped through to the happy, all-the-children-safely-home end, and we looked for another book.

Bloodless retellings are cursed enough, but worse has fallen upon the old, true story. In our modern world, Peter Pan is, if not quite abhorred, a shameful sort of being. We have the "Peter Pan syndrome," the condition of so many painfully immature men—the uncommitted lovers, the bad fathers, the men who leave stinky socks and soda cans lying around for someone else (a Wendy-woman) to pick up. We have pathetic Michael Jackson, who adopted Peter Pan as his own frightening persona and has the disfigured nose to go with it. He has forever and ever sullied not just Peter's innocence but the magic of Neverland, hijacked from our imaginations to his own corrupt fantasies. Even the mysterious J. M. Barrie has now been exposed, in a movie devoted to his own peculiar life, as a stunted adult given to playing with little boys and, like a little boy himself, in need of mothering.

⁂

I cling to my Neverland and its inhabitants, as I knew them. I never come upon a hollowed cottonwood tree without wanting to tuck myself inside and slide through into Peter's world. Fireflies are as astonishing as fairies, and the stars still beckon. Large furry dogs and wind-up alarm clocks will always be more than dogs and clocks. I search my maps for lagoons, still enchanted with the word, still watching for mermaids and pirate ships or whatever might be found there. One of my early, happiest jobs in Alaska was at a fish hatchery in an actual lagoon—Tutka Bay Lagoon—as magical a place as might exist in the physical world, where tides poured like a river through its hidden entrance and we gathered Dungeness crabs from the shoreline for dinner, where the calm water was dark with swirling schools of salmon and the surrounding forest, thick in mossy trees, creaked in the wind.

It's at night, dreaming, that I most achingly return to Neverland. All these years later, the Peter dreams still come. In them, I know just how to lift my arms and wiggle my shoulders. All of the earth's weightedness leaves me as I float away, through the branches of giant oaks, over rooftops and foamy seas and the green swaths of bucolic countryside — all the iconic landscapes of the known earth. I dance through air, hovering with a swish of hands and a paddle of feet. I kick out and head for the stars.

The voices are with me there still, a chorus of voices escalating into high and delirious notes: "I'm flying!" "I'm flying!" "I'm flying!!"

In those dreams, I'm as bird-weight as a child, as fearless and sure, as free and unto myself as I can possibly be. I feel it in my body — the breeze on my skin, the lift, the turn of my shoulders as I lay myself out flat. I'm flying, I'm free, I'm still — to use Mark Twain's phrase — "lighting out for the territory."

When I wake the sensation stays with me, and I know that in some sense that's essentially real, I was flying.

჻

Who was that child? She was someone who found what she needed in a book and in the boundless play of childhood. And what was that — that thing she needed and found? It was — I think I can put it simply — *an enlargement*. Ordinary life is small; the life of the imagination is vast. I can do anything, be anything, think anything. I can go anywhere, even real places, and find a real home large and unruly enough to contain me and what I might make of its saved, scavenged, and utterly unexpected but essential parts. I might, even as an adult, using words, toss up some handfuls of fairy dust to scatter in the wind.

ON REREADING SIDDHARTHA

LUCKY FOR ME, growing into the restlessness of my teen-
aged years, I was allowed to abandon the public school and
teachers I blamed — with all the contemptuousness of an
impatient and intolerant thirteen-year-old — for "wast-
ing my time." A new, private, college-prep school was just
opening as I entered eighth grade, and my parents were
both able and willing to pay the tuition. Who's to say what
might have become of me had I not had this privileged
option? I tend to think I would have joined the class of
bright dropouts who settle for a GED and then find their
ways (or not) to some level of self-education and intellectual challenge. I might — who knows? — have run off
to Alaska at an early age.

In any case, eighth grade found me happily ensconced
in a school temporarily housed in a downtown Boy's Club,
thinking like mad. My brain stretched around Latin and

French, mathematical proofs, history as story (in contrast to memorized dates), and the art and wisdom of Shakespeare and Homer and Hesse.

Hesse?

I don't know why our English teacher presented us with Hermann Hesse's *Siddhartha*. The story of a Brahmin's son who goes off to find the meaning of life was not a logical fit for even a private school in a conservative New Hampshire town still largely untouched by the spirit of the 1960s. Other eighth-graders read, I think, books like *David Copperfield*, *The Catcher in the Rye*, and *To Kill a Mockingbird* — wonderful books, and revolutionary in their own ways, but more standard for the times, more of a piece with the culture in which we were assumed to live. Before being presented with the small paperback, I certainly had never heard of Hesse. None of us, I think, had had any introduction to German writers, Romanticism or neo-Romanticism, or eastern religions. We might barely have understood something about allegory.

※

More than three decades later, while browsing in the town library adjacent to a writers' colony where I was "in residence," my eye fell upon a slim blue book, jacketless and worn, with silver letters shining from its spine. I believe in library angels, or whatever it is that directs you to shelves and launches books into your hands, that causes pages bearing information you must have but don't know you're looking for to fly open before you. *Siddhartha* came to me, musty, with rounded corners and a loose binding, with an egg-blue spiral penned on its back endpaper. I flipped pages, saw the familiar name Govinda, saw references to Buddha and a ferry. The story began to come back.

I checked out the book, took it to my writers' colony room, sat in an armchair under good light, and read it through, as an old, bifocaled woman of forty-six years. I was significantly older than my teacher would have been when he chose it as a text. I was as old as my parents had been when I studied *Siddhartha* under their sheltering roof. I was, I saw, when I looked up Hesse's birthdate, already a year older than Hesse had been when *Siddhartha* was first published.

I often reread books. I've returned to *Moby-Dick*, *The Scarlet Letter*, *Lolita*, finding each richer in repetition. I regularly reread Chekhov's "The Lady with the Dog," Thurber's "The Catbird Seat," and Welty's "The Worn Path," bolstered each time by their power and beauty. But I had not read *Siddhartha*, or anything else by Hermann Hesse, since that heady high-school time of intellectual and self-discovery, when I had begun with *Siddhartha* and read, as though I were sucking up oxygen, a steady flow of Hesse's novels. Those books belonged to a time I wasn't sure I wanted to disturb. But I was curious, too. I wanted to know if *Siddhartha* was a good book. I wanted to know if it had, as I suspected was possible, changed my life.

❧

My eighth-grade English teacher was a man named Jack Coogan — *Mr.* Coogan to us. He smoked a pipe and somehow — in his bearing and his passions for literature, for the task of teaching, and even, it seemed, for those of us who fell under his charge — commanded our respect. I think of him as old, although he was not. He had young children then and taught school for another thirty years.

In a school as small as ours, the English department consisted of Mr. Coogan and perhaps one or two others. Thus it was that I studied English, literature, writing, and various related electives under the same Mr. Coogan for most of my high school years. My memory mixes and mashes, but I do recall with fondness an early text called *Sound & Sense*, discovering the playful poetry of e. e. cummings, acting out scenes from Arthur Miller's *The Crucible*. That eighth-grade year I remember such a small thing as learning to mark passages in books that were not school district property but my own to annotate and love. In a short-story anthology, I had used a ruler to neatly underline sentences and whole paragraphs that seemed to me to hold particular significance; I'd circled every unfamiliar word and printed its definition at the bottom of its page. Mr. Coogan sat with me one day and told me to forget ruler and precision. He demonstrated through several pages, roughly bracketing passages, scribbling key words, leaving questions to return to. I learned, in that five-minute tutorial, how to be an active, critical, free-wheeling reader.

Somewhere in those years I remember Mr. Coogan challenging us with the question, *does reading constitute experience?* Can you be affected by something you read in the same way or to the same end as you might be by actual flesh-and-blood experience? I don't remember any of us taking him up on the challenge, but I do remember him asking the question more than once and looking frustrated when he couldn't get an argument out of us, either way. By then it must have been the late sixties, and we must, as a class, have fallen into the pessimism of the age and our own teenage madness.

I would not myself have responded. Those years, for reasons I don't yet understand and probably never will, I was practically mute in class. Speaking in groups didn't come naturally to me, and, though I knew I should make the effort, I simply didn't. I think this was not a matter of self-confidence, as the disparity between male and female class participation is commonly explained today, but something deeper. I didn't fear I would say something stupid, because I knew I was not stupid. I was thinking all the time, taking in what I read and heard and ordering it for my own uses, but I didn't feel obliged to project my thoughts into the classroom. I submitted superior analytical papers and creative work, but I did not speak. I think, perhaps, I was preparing to be a writer, though I didn't know then that I even wanted to be one.

These days, when I stand in front of students and talk, I don't know where that ability comes from, or when it came to me. Very often, there's one (usually female) student listening quietly, and I'm torn between wanting her to speak — because that makes the teacher's work easier — and respecting her silence.

§

In my armchair at the writers' colony, I read: "In the shade of the house, in the sunshine on the river bank by the boats, in the shade of the sallow wood and the fig tree, Siddhartha, the handsome Brahmin's son, grew up with his friend Govinda."

On Rereading Siddhartha | 19

These words fell upon me with a great, good, heart-warming sense of familiarity. They are simple words, scented with exotic promise, entering the world with rhythmic ease. They were familiar not because I remembered them — a passage I might once have underlined — but because I have long since internalized the simplicity of that language and the serial phrasing that makes for such lyrical, rolling, grace. In my writerly dreams, I would write like this.

The story, for those who will not have read or remembered it, follows the young Siddhartha from his departure from home (where he bests his father in a test of wills — yahoo!), through his years wandering with a band of ascetics (rejecting all material comfort) to his meeting with Buddha (whom he declines to follow, although his friend Govinda does) and his entry into the world of sexual pleasure, business, money, and possessions, to his flight from that empty life (despair, suicidal thoughts) to a river, where he meets an enlightened ferryman who teaches him to listen to the river and whom he then joins in that simple life, from which he is eventually jostled by the appearance of the son (begat with his courtesan-lover during his profligate days) whom he fails, despite his new-found capacity to love, to win over. In the end, Siddhartha, a wise and maybe holy old man, again meets with his friend Govinda, to whom he displays his saintliness but, pointedly, imparts no doctrine.

It was clear to me, rereading Siddhartha, why the story appealed to me so much in my youth. Didn't I also resist the conventionality of my family and what I saw as the smallness of the lives surrounding me, and didn't I also yearn to head out on my own, to live a life of spiritual awareness and intellectual mindfulness?

Although for a time Siddhartha gave in to the seductions of material culture and the unthinking people who were like children, he recovered from that and found his way again by listening to the river. I knew how to listen to rivers; I knew that nature was the only god worth listening to. Raised in the Protestant Church, I disliked the way that Christianity (and all other religions of which I knew) forced upon its believers "thou shalt not" laws, rather than encouraging independent thought or allowing for ambiguity.

Love was hard, Siddhartha learned, and came paired with pain. I could accept that, as I could wonder with the young Siddhartha whether I was even capable of love.

Listen to the river. Listen to yourself. No one else — not parents, not teachers, not best friends, not even the great Buddha himself — has answers for you. What you need in life will not be taught but must be learned, and learning comes from the active pursuit of knowledge, of oneself and of the world.

What a message to impart to restless, eager, arrogantly doubting teenagers! How had this thin, translated-from-the-German fairytale of a book, written in the ancient year of 1922 by the son of Pietistic Lutheran missionaries, a school dropout, a failed suicide, a Jungian, and a poet, come to my classroom and to the hearts and minds of so many rebellious or reflective children of the 1960s? Although I didn't know it then, *Siddhartha* was being discovered and embraced by young people all across the country; it was or would become a classic of the age. We sixties children were all, it seemed — like Siddhartha — the ultimate outsiders.

Then, though, my context was small. In the self-absorbed fashion of thirteen-year-olds, I felt that my response, what the book meant to *me*, was everything. I'm sure Mr. Coogan must have talked to us about Hesse and the tradition of German Romanticism, about Hinduism and Buddhism, and about narrative, allegory, myth-making, and the literature of questing. Surely we looked at the construction of the story, at symbols, and at the lovely, lilting prose, the simple language that, nevertheless, conveyed large ideas. Surely we wrote papers on some aspect or another. I remember none of this.

What I remember is the *feeling*, the sense the book instilled in me, that there was beauty in language and strength in ideas, however fictional might be their cloak. I could immerse myself in text and feel at home there, in a world that was bigger and more promising and other than anything I'd yet met. I was affirmed in the present by something that dwelt in foreign lands and times of old, something that, even so, seemed to explain *me*.

Siddhartha "looked around him as if seeing the world for the first time." Siddhartha listened to the river and understood how everything flowed together. Siddhartha saw that people were like falling leaves, except for the few who were like stars traveling one defined path, untouched by wind, with their guide and path within. I had had those moments. Yes, I identified. I would not be a falling leaf.

I reached the part, in my rereading, about Kamala, the beautiful courtesan. I read of her "bright red mouth like a freshly cut fig," and I remembered the simile as though I'd written it myself. I think in fact I *did* write it. A vague recollection came back to me, of choosing Kamala for a writing assignment, beginning with her fig lips and writing her life as she, not Siddhartha, might have known it. I hadn't identified with Kamala, I think, as I had with Siddhartha, but I had liked the power she wielded as a woman. She was not the toy of slobby men, not inferior, not victim, but a courtesan who chose her lovers and practiced with and upon them a high art. That I knew nothing firsthand of sex had not, I think, detracted from my appreciation of sexual power.

※

A few months before *Siddhartha* sprang at me from a library shelf, a close friend from my high school years — of whom I'd had no news at all in the intervening decades — found me on the Internet. His e-mail subject line, "This was not written by Hermann Hesse," had sent blood pounding into my head. I was no longer a Hessophile, had not thought about any of Hesse's characters or themes in I didn't know how long. I'd certainly thought of my friend from time to time, but I had completely forgotten, until Hesse's name appeared before me in twelve-point font, that I had insisted he read *Siddhartha* and *Steppenwolf* and I don't know what all else.

At that time of my life, I had collected and shared everything I could find by Hesse. The titles, if not the storylines, still roll off my tongue: *The Glass Bead Game, Narcissus and Goldmund, Demian, Beneath the Wheel, Rosshalde, Klingsor's Last Summer, The Journey to the East.* I had worked studiously through at least one book of Hessian criticism — not for any class, but in my own pursuit of knowledge.

When I was a high school junior or senior, on the last day of school, I remember pawing through piles of books and papers that students had flung from their lockers, collecting the copies of *Siddhartha* left behind by that year's eighth-graders. I was offended by their abandonment and the state of their torn pages and defaced covers, and I rescued what I could in the belief that they should find better appreciation elsewhere. I passed them on to those who needed them, just as evangelicals pressed their tracts upon those they would save.

When my friend thought of me all these years later, he thought of Hesse. I must have been fanatical.

꙳

After Kamala, after his business and gambling ventures, Siddhartha came once again to the river. The river spoke to him with the perfect sound of *Om*, and he embraced the world afresh, with the innocence of a child.

> He looked lovingly into the flowing water, into the transparent green, into the crystal lines of its wonderful design. He saw bright pearls rise from the depths, bubbles swimming on the mirror, sky blue reflected in them. . . . He saw that the river continually flowed and flowed and yet it was always there; it was always the same and yet every moment it was new. Who could understand, conceive this? He did not understand it; he was only aware of a dim suspicion, a faint memory, divine voices.

I remembered, well enough, going into the world under this influence. Consciously I accepted what I found there, as a child would. (The fact that I was still largely a child perhaps escaped me.)

Here's what I want to know, though: to what extent did *Siddhartha* influence me philosophically, and to what extent did it simply match my own affinity? Clearly I was predisposed to hear the message. Otherwise *Siddhartha* would long ago have washed through the sieve of my memory like so much else I read at the time. We made a pair, that book and I. And not only content-wise. Lean prose is much my own style, and lyricism my ideal. But how much is influence, how much convergence?

At the least, there is something to be said for validation. It's always a pleasure to find the questionable workings of your own mind reinforced. At age thirteen, when you fear you might be the only out-of-step dancer in the universe, that affirmation can be a soul-saver. I needed what *Siddhartha* delivered — a bolstering of my idea of myself and the life worth living, life that involved intellect and art and living close to nature, as simply and usefully as ferrymen.

As luck would have it, the library angels visited me once more, and delivered to my hands Hesse's own answer to the question of influence. In *Reflections*, a hagiological book of Hesse quotations, I found this: "Our inner compass is deflected by every book we read; every outside mind shows us from how many other points of view the world can be considered. Then the oscillation gradually dies down, and the needle returns to its old orientation, inherent in the nature of each one of us."

Except, I think — to extend the metaphor — sometimes, when we strike metals that have for us the right magnetic charge, our inner compass might forever be moved by a degree or two. *Siddhartha*, as one work of art that carried that particular charge for me, taught me about ways of seeing, the value of patience, the importance of rightly chosen words and artful phrasings. These were wrapped up together, sound and sense, forming an aesthetic that before or after, egg or chicken, was and became and is my own. The whole concept of an inner compass — that, too, was something I'd known. Had I not, in Alaska, drawn the title of my first story collection from another quotation about a compass? In naming *The Compass Inside Ourselves*, I'd responded to a beloved writer, Eudora Welty, and her use of the phrase to acknowledge both our home ties and our spiritual homes. I meant to honor my origins — which included the book-places where I'd felt I belonged — and the home of my spirit and my stories, Alaska.

At dinner at the writing colony, I asked my fellow residents, "Did you ever read *Siddhartha*?" Most had — several with enthusiasm, none with less than a general if vague fondness. Those older than I had come to the little book in their twenties, glad for its spiritual steadiness; the youngest among us, thirtysomething, had read it, like me, as a school assignment. I hadn't realized quite how cultishly popular, how much a part of the larger culture *Siddhartha* had been. I was, maybe, disappointed — because, wasn't *I* really different?

Did anyone still read Hesse? Except for one woman who periodically returned to *Demian*, none of us did; we agreed he seemed to have fallen from fashion. I, despite my one-time devotion, had obviously not made a career out of Hessian scholarship, had never even made much of an exploration into related matters — eastern religions, for example, or Jungian psychology. After high school, the doors to learning had swung so wide for me, I'd spread myself with what might have seemed a random scrabbling, one enthusiasm leading to the next. I didn't much, in the ensuing years, come across references to Hesse, and I don't recall ever engaging in conversation about him or his works. I had not recently witnessed any young people trotting past with *Steppenwolf* clutched to their chests.

There is one sure way to test trends, and the next day I took a look on the Internet. A Siddhartha search led to sites belonging to a Siddhartha School, online bookstores from which *Siddhartha* could be ordered, and real-life people named Siddhartha. A Hermann Hesse search found a Web magazine published at the University of California at Santa Barbara, the primary purpose of which is to list Hesse events taking place around the world — a conference on Romanticism, an exhibit of Hesse's watercolor paintings, the meeting schedule of a Japanese club that studies German literature.

At Amazon.com I found 128 items by and about the man, including *Siddhartha* on audio cassette, a recent biography (*Hermann Hesse: Pilgrim of Crisis*) and an even newer book of criticism (*Understanding*

Hermann Hesse: The Man, His Myth, His Metaphor). There was, even at the end of the twentieth century, a Hesse industry. I had a fleeting vision of middle-aged corporate commuters pushing *Siddhartha* into their SUV tape players for a ride into the countryside.

I looked to see how well *Siddhartha*, the book, was selling. The Amazon sales rank was 3,581. Not bad, I thought. Sixty-two customers had posted reviews and given it an average grade of four and a half stars. I browsed the most recently posted reviews.

From California: "Much better than I'd thought it'd be. I had to read this book for my 9th grade English class. Although the premise was a little confusing, I liked how it showed all of the facets of a balanced life, in Hesse's opinion. I had recently thought of myself as a horrible person, because I tend to think about things differently than other people, but this book changed my opinion of myself for a few hours. I recommend this book to anyone who has a lot of time on their hands, and wants to ponder the meaning of life."

From Japan: "This is the first book I fell in love with."

From Idaho: "This book is great! You could really learn a lot from this book. The journey is so symbolic and the transcendental references are outstanding!"

From New Zealand: "It has given my life a spiritual lift and has really changed my tone of thought."

Young people were reading *Siddhartha*. Not as many as were reading *The Catcher in the Rye* (ranked at 219, with 364 posted reviews), but what seemed to me a significant number, significantly moved. I felt truly and deeply cheered.

༅

In the end, when Siddhartha and Govinda are reunited, Siddhartha picks up a stone. "This," he said, handling it,

> is a stone, and within a certain length of time it will perhaps be soil and from the soil it will become plant, animal or man . . . I do not respect and love it because it was one thing and will become something else, but because it has already long been everything and

always is everything. I love it just because it is a stone, because today and now it appears to me a stone. I see value and meaning in each one of its fine markings and cavities, in the yellow, in the gray, in the hardness and the sound of it when I knock it, in the dryness or dampness of its surface . . . But I will say no more about it. Words do not express thoughts very well. They always become a little different immediately they are expressed, a little distorted, a little foolish. And yet it also pleases me and seems right that what is of value and wisdom to one man seems nonsense to another.

This little speech does not, in my middle-age, seem to me either simplistic or juvenile. To me, it makes great good sense, respectful of the earth and all its mysteries, including the minds of other people. I've become — or perhaps always was — a great fondler of stones, as happy as Siddhartha with the way they feel in my hands and how the light shines upon them. I'm less accepting, I know, of those who would see nonsense where I see value, but then, I'm not as wise yet as I might still become.

๛

Mr. Coogan, clever teacher that he was, wanted us to think about literature as life experience, about how what we read might influence our lives. Does reading constitute experience? Might what happens between book and mind compare to what happens between a more direct sensory acquaintance with the world and that same mind?

All these years later, I'm still thinking this over. Reading about getting hit by a truck is not, of course, the same as getting hit by a truck. But we all — those of us who read — know about the fabulous entry books give us into other minds, times, cultures, layers of experience we could never be otherwise allowed, whether we wanted to go there in person or not. Some of these slip away from us rather quickly, like dreams, into unconsciousness or oblivion. Others resonate for a good long time.

As the young Californian reported to Amazon, *Siddhartha* changed his opinion of himself for a few hours. That, I suppose, is a long time in our fast-paced present.

I'm convinced that the right books catch us, as the right teachers and friends do, at the right, ready, needy moments in our lives. We may need to hear from Jo in *Little Women*, from Holden Caulfield or the Karamazov brothers or the mysterious Emily Dickinson. When the books come to us, we recognize them. Once met, they stay with us forever, whether we know it or not, in the deepest determinations of who we are and how we respond to the rest of what life brings us.

I think about Mr. Coogan's question, and it's like a Zen koan, a question with no logical solution. The answer is not an answer at all but a meditation. I may or may not have begun to learn this from Hesse and *Siddhartha* in the eighth grade, but I continue to learn it every day of my life: what's worth seeking isn't answers, but questions. I trust more than anything that the art of living, like the art of writing, lies in the framing of questions and in their turning, again and again, like stones in our hands, all through our thinking lives.

IN THE GIANT'S HAND

ARRIGETCH, I KNEW BEFORE I FIRST ARRIVED in
Alaska, meant "fingers of the hand extended" in the language of the Nunamiut people, the inland Eskimos who
once broadly inhabited the land. The Arrigetch peaks in
Alaska's central Brooks Range were anomalous gray granite
upthrusts, mountaineers' hard-rock dreams, as dramatic a
landscape as can be found anywhere on earth.

Today, their photographs grace one nature calendar
after another, and a national park — Gates of the Arctic — surrounds them, the sparkliest jewel cluster in a
many-jeweled crown. But in 1971, the Arrigetch were still
off the maps of most Americans, still part of that great
wild north that, even on real, topographic maps, existed
only at the 1:250,000 scale. An inch spanned four miles,
and still there were broad blank spaces marked only with
contour lines and the earth colors of vegetation and rock.

The blue threads of unnamed creeks wound through unnamed valleys under unnamed mountains, and there was nothing like a road or airstrip or even a trail in sight. The Brooks and the Arrigetch were epic countries then, places of outermost dream. They were the possibility I'd been searching for forever, or at least for the dozen or more years that I'd been longing for distance and wildness.

⚜

A June day, that ancient year. The sky is blue. The air is warm. For the moment, there's enough breeze to keep most of the mosquitoes grounded in the tightly woven tundra. Snow patches still fill hollows and streak the north-facing slopes, but they're melting as I watch, tinkling as their skeletal crystals collapse against rock. Green spears and tiny, pastel alpine flowers rush to fill in behind the retreating snow. It's all like some heavenly garden as I work my way along the pathways of licheny rock slabs and nappy ground, down from the benchland where our tents flutter their bright primary colors, to the valley floor and the creek that creases its bottom. Rivulets of water run everywhere, down the faces of rocks, into cascading waterfalls, spilling from one basin into the next. Small birds flit, and bees buzz. One solitary caribou lifts its alert head and springs away on clicking hooves. The air is so incredibly clear, like looking through ice water — it almost magnifies. Those silvery granite peaks rise all around, as though just yesterday some god or giant pushed them through the crust. Rumblings of rockfall attest to the work-in-progress nature of this nature; freeze and thaw, freeze and thaw, and gravity exerting its pull. Talus stacks up deeply, precariously, at the mountains' feet.

I climb to the top of a boulder and spread myself over its sun-warmed surface. It pleases me to believe, true or not, that I could be the first person ever to climb up and sit on top of this particular rock. I suspect that Native hunters didn't do a lot of frivolous rock-sitting, and few other people have entered here — to my knowledge only one previous group of recreationalists. Everything about the entire valley and surrounding peaks, sky, and last, lost, never-never land pleases me; if I had to construct an image of paradise, this would be it.

From the distance comes the clear, clean, ringing sound of a piton being pounded into rock. Others of my party have availed themselves of the practice cliffs close to camp, to test the rock and their own climbing skills. We are here, after all, as climbers — ten of us from a new little college in Massachusetts: two who teach in the school's Outdoors Program, the wife of one, and seven students who have just completed their own and the college's first year. Our leader, David Roberts, a veteran of numerous Alaska climbing expeditions, had taught us, back in the smoothed-over Berkshires, the rudimentary arts of negotiating rock walls and had now brought us to a place of Olympian proportion. David was, at the time, only twenty-seven years old. When I think back from an age when anyone *under* thirty seems suspect, at the least frighteningly short on maturity — I'm astonished. Who allowed us all to go off and do something so grand?

Lest you think some disaster befell us, let me assure you that it did not. For five weeks the ten of us climbed, hiked, camped among bears, and swirled downriver in plastic rafts, and we suffered nothing worse than blisters, mosquito bites, and the occasional storm of irritation with one another.

It could have been otherwise, which was part of the attraction. We were in wilderness in a time before global positioning systems and personal rescue beacons that report via satellite, never mind satellite telephones. We carried a substantial rifle — a 30.06 — for bear protection, but no radio of any kind. Had any of us fallen sick or been injured, the closest help lay two days distant. There was not, in those days, even much plane traffic; in our weeks in the Arrigetch, the only plane we saw was the one that made our airdrop onto a rock field, bursting our boxes and spraying our one bag of sugar into oblivion.

David much later reminded me that, of everyone on that trip, I was the only one who approached Alaska as something more than an attractive summer playground. He remembered me going on, like someone immodestly in love, about how fabulous the country was, how paradisiacal, how there could be no other place on earth so exactly what I considered ideal and idyllic. I reminded David that, when I packed up and moved to Alaska two years later, he had warned me against doing so. What he'd said was, *living in Alaska will rot your brain*. He'd meant, Alaska was a place of pure physicality, where people merely survived, largely by drinking; his visits — even a stint of university teaching — hadn't led him to believe there was any cultural, intellectual, or social life worth living in such a void. Grudgingly, David had to admit that, for me, there *was* something more.

⚬

See me there, on top of that unsullied boulder, filling my whole self with that pure Alaska spring air, my heart so big in my chest it might push right through my ribs. See me leap down and nearly weep at the flutter of bell-shaped flowers. I drink of the running water, gaze at the lofty peaks, dream of remaining forever in that perfect valley.

Am I over the top in my enthusiasms? Absolutely. Even as I fantasize staying in the Arrigetch for all time, I must know that the brief summer interlude is just that, and that Arctic winters are interminably long, sunlessly dark, and spit-freezingly cold. Still I hold an image of myself curled up in an earthen house under caribou blankets, savoring moonlight and sculpted snowdrifts.

⚬

I was not really a climber. I had learned to enjoy attacking rock like a puzzle, trusting my body to find handholds and fist-jamming cracks, to stand on my feet. I was reasonably fearless when belayed from above, willing to try any move, capable of finding my way up easy routes. I liked the teamwork, the coaching and coaxing, the feel of rope at my waist and, while belaying another, feeding assuredly through my hands. I liked simply being on rock, pressing palm and fingertips to the grainy surface, admiring the way plants worked tenacious roots into the smallest cracks on the tiniest ledges; I loved, in the Arrigetch, being surprised by an exquisitely white snow bunting that shot out of its nest near the top of a cliff. But I was not ambitious when it came to climbing, and not particularly competitive. I had no great desires to reach the tops of those granite fingers — except, perhaps, to see over the other side, to gaze upon more of my beloved land.

I did climb some, there in the Arrigetch. I practiced on the cliffs and on boulders, and I partook of the one climb we all did together — up to the col between two peaks named the East and West Maidens, where we split into four groups, two for each peak. I summited the East Maiden, not much of a technical feat. We might have simply walked the ridge, but we were cautious; we roped up and protected the route. At the top we found the cairn and bottled note of the only previous ascenders, from 1964. The view of the vertical back side made me hold my breath — that deep dive to another green and river-braided valley and, beyond, more rows of blue mountains fading gradually to pale and paler, turning under with the earth's very curve. We ate our candy bars and retreated. Clouds moved in, and snow flurried down on us. We retraced our chopped steps down a long snow couloir and picked our way back over a longer and shifty boulder field.

Other days, with various combinations of companions, I explored our valley, hiked to another col between two peaks, hiked to the pass at the head of the valley. The day that David and Ed Ward, our other climbing instructor, made a first ascent of a monolith called Shot Tower, I hiked to its base to watch them negotiate its difficult midsection. Back at camp, near midnight, I watched with binoculars as they, tiny as flies in the dome of a cathedral, finally stood on top and waved. In my innocence, I had never doubted that they would.

Four of us organized a five-day trek, from our valley over the pass, through the next valley and back to camp, about a twenty-five-mile circuit. We saw small numbers of caribou and traveled, at times, on their grooved trails lined with discarded antlers and dry bones, bits of caribou hair blowing in the breeze. Aside from another cairn and note at the top of the pass, left by the same party that had climbed the Maidens in '64, we saw no other sign of humans, not so much as a jet's contrail overhead. Laboring under my pack through heat, thunderstorm, and mosquitoes, I lost myself in the idea of valley after splendorous valley. We forded creeks and bathed in pools, studied our map and located the right pass to complete our circle. The last day we found ourselves deep in bushwhacking country, with no animal trails through the tangles and mosquitoes so thick we could kill forty with a swat. I thought I might die. But then we climbed out of the brush and the bugs, back to base camp, that place that still looked a lot like heaven.

⚜

I kept a journal that summer, a journal I didn't look at again until I decided to try this essay — only to discover that the pages were filled with overwrought teenage emotion rather than useful detail. I did not record the name of a single plant (except the fabulous fireweed) or bird (not even the snow bunting) or any other bit of natural history smaller than caribou. I also did not take any photos that summer — or even own a camera. The life of the moment was all I wanted, and I was sure that such moments would be mine forever — because I would never forget, and because I would return to the Arrigetch many more times. I would become, I wrote in my journal, a park ranger or an archaeologist or a camp cook.

My one concession to naming things lies at the heart of my journal — a map I drew of our valley, showing the circling of peaks, each with the name bestowed by climbers before us and known to David — Citadel, the Camel, Disneyland, Badile, Battleship, Pyramid, the Prong, sixteen altogether on my map. I show the creek running down the center of the valley, the pass at the head, and our four tents pitched on the bench below the Maidens. It's a fair representation, I think, and in my head today stands for the place itself, which otherwise would be far vaguer, shrouded in forgetful mist.

⚜

After three weeks in the mountains, we packed up our tents, sleeping bags, and climbing hardware, hoisted our loads, and hiked out, three days to a lake where we traded our mountaineering gear for plastic rafts with wimpy toy paddles. For ten days a slow current carried us down 180 miles of winding Alatna River. Fireweed blazed along the banks, we napped, we swam, we watched two young wolves playing. It rained, and we gathered around a driftwood fire and got smoke in our eyes while we ate more noodles with tuna and described for one another the tastes of fresh apples, peaches, asparagus. We reached a village with a volleyball court and an airstrip, and we got on a scheduled plane and flew to Fairbanks and drove back to Massachusetts.

᯼

Two years later, with my fisherman-wannabe sweetie, I moved to Alaska. Ken and I chose as home nowhere near my perfect and implausible Arrigetch, but a town on the south coast; its dot on a map, at the end of a road, looked of a size that seemed "right" if you expected to find some kind of existing shelter, someone to pay you for doing something, and a post office where you might have an address. We've lived there ever since, with summers at our fish camp across the inlet, and I've never returned to the Arrigetch or anywhere at all in the Brooks Range.

If you'd told me in 1971 that I wouldn't see the Arrigetch again, I would not have believed you. What, short of death, would keep me away?

The truth is, the reality of living in Alaska impressed itself upon me rather quickly. In our seasonal economy, summer is the frantic period in which to work and earn money; one doesn't go off and scamper in the mountains. I also learned something about the rest of the year. Winter has its pleasures, but huddling in the cold and dark are not among them. Somehow, I did not become a mountain-mama outdoorswoman, and I did not build my own little log cabin in the Arctic, or even in the sub-Arctic. I did, for a couple of summers, become a camp cook and then a "fish tech" at a salmon hatchery, where I filled my spare time fishing for Dolly Varden and picking blueberries by the bucket. Ken and I *did* take up commercial salmon fishing and get to know our length of fishing beach and its inhabitants with considerable intimacy, and I *have* seen much of the rest of Alaska's magnificent coastline. I *have* fallen in love with landscapes all over the state, from southeast forests to Alaska Peninsula volcanoes to barrier islands along the Arctic coast. Every day, when I look out my Homer window at ocean, mountains, and sky, I marvel at the beauty I live within.

In the Giant's Hand | 35

I know that, although I could, I probably never will see the Arrigetch again. But I'm all right with that. I know something that I didn't know when I was nineteen, and it has to do with the limits of one life. I also know better some things I may have known even at nineteen, having to do with seizing opportunities and letting ourselves dream. The power of the Arrigetch, for me, lay not only in its splendor, its scale, and the possibilities it suggested. The Arrigetch impressed upon me the potency of place and the need for large landscapes that will forever be *more* than what we humans want to make of them. I will forever, as long as I live, advocate the protection of such places — the Arctic National Wildlife Refuge, the Bristol Bay watershed, free-running rivers, roadless forests with gnarly old trees, oceans of fish — even as others attempt to reap another kind of riches from those places. Our children and their children need those places left whole. Numberless generations are yet to find their own imaginative homes, their own limits. Our planet — now more than ever — needs to retain natural systems and a diversity of species, as its very lifeblood.

A life in Alaska has left me without delusion or much sentiment. Each new summer I meet young people backpacking through town, turning their ruddy faces to the hills. I overhear their plans for scaling this or running that and how, later, they'll find some old cabin to make over for winter. They talk about Lake Clark and Katmai, about Denali, the Wrangells, and Kenai Fjords. They get out their maps and find the big spaces that still exist. At the end of the road and beyond, the newly arrived lie down in fields of fireweed or walk barefoot on smooth sand beaches, and they think they've found the places that will forever set the standards for what's loveliest and most necessary in the world. Each new summer I find myself smiling. I know the innocents are dreaming and will likely be gone before the first frost. And that's all right. We don't really want all those people living in Alaska. What matters is that they learn what's possible, and something about beauty, and what it is to live under a mountain or by a river, in the hands of whatever giant they might imagine, and that they carry that knowledge and spirit into memory, into the rest of their lives.

IN THE COUNTRY

Everything is flowing — going

somewhere, animals and so-called

lifeless rocks as well as water.

JOHN MUIR

WORDS HONOR PLACE

Almost at every moment in time, notably in the sphere of
American Indian speech, some ancient and rich expression
of articulate being is lapsing into irretrievable silence.
GEORGE STEINER, *AFTER BABEL*, 1975

AS I WALKED ONE DAY through woods above my fish
camp, I found myself thinking of the stream that slipped
by me in the brush. Although I only glimpsed it in one
spot, I knew its twists and turns as contours of the place,
its flow not just as water but as map. This, after all — this
movement of water — was the traditional way by which
the people of the place knew where they were and where
they were going.

Before the invention of compasses, people in most parts
of the world marked direction by the sun and stars. In the
far north, though, the sun crosses the sky in greatly varied
locations depending on the season, and summer nights are
too light for spotting stars. In Alaska, the Yupiit and Inupiat
of the coastal regions developed directional systems based
on positions relative to the coastline, while the Athabascans
developed theirs according to the flow of rivers.

The logic of this — even for me, who came to the Alaska shore from afar and only as an adult — is obvious, and truly lovely. The old, meandering trail above my camp keeps the creek on one side, connects the beach on Cook Inlet with the forested uplands. Downstream the creek takes me home, upstream it takes me to ponds and a lake; upstream the lake takes me further inland to another lake. Since the beginning of our lives here Ken and I have referred to Cook Inlet itself in upstream and downstream terms, because of the way the water flows in and rushes out on the tides. When I learned that the Dena'ina Athabascans who first inhabited the Cook Inlet area called the inlet something that translated to "Big-water River" and marked its directions as upstream, downstream, and across, I understood with new clarity how the language was confirming the landscape, the landscape shaping the language. The way of speaking about the inlet was given by the inlet itself.

Later, as I learned a small amount of Dena'ina vocabulary and language structure, I began to see ways in which the entire Dena'ina language system reflects a profound dependence on locations. Athabascan languages layer prefixes and suffixes onto root words in a way that emphasizes directions, placements, distances, and relative positioning. The complexity of this emphasis in a semi-nomadic culture where people needed to be very clear about where they were and where they needed to go for food and other necessities might be compared to the complexity of verb tenses in the languages of cultures oriented more toward considerations of time and timing. The Dena'ina language, with its system of building short and precise locational words, serves life in its place both efficiently and elegantly.

Languages, of course, belong to environments in the very same way that living creatures do. They're indigenous to the places that spawn them, both in the words needed to identify and address the particulars of those places and in the structure needed to survive in them. The smatterings of European languages I've learned at one time or another have always offered me insights into the ways people of different cultures have thought about themselves, what those cultures have valued, how they fit their origins. That certain nouns are designated as masculine and others feminine, that the Russians have a single word for *happiness* and *luck* — these are salient indicators of how people adapted to their surroundings, of how they still think about themselves and their places in the world.

And so, quite naturally, I wanted to learn what I could of the language of the place where I live, just as I want to know its plants and wildlife. Until very recently, the area around my fish camp had been little affected by the industrialism of the last two centuries. It remains home to trees, water, weather, fish, and bears, and so the language that evolved in it surely still connects in deep ecological patterns, tying nature to culture, culture to nature. The very name of its foreland — *Kustatan*, "point of land" — describes it perfectly. The brown bear's name — *ggagga* — is used sometimes to refer to animals in general and indicates just how significant the brown bear was in Dena'ina culture; this reminds me always that bears are still largely in charge at Kustatan, and of the respect due them. The raven's name is *ggugguyni*, pronounced to match the watery gurgle the bird makes in the back of its own throat, and the golden-crowned sparrow — *tsik'ezlagh* — all summer sings the three descending minor-key notes that sound out its name. My experience of what I see and hear around me is vastly enriched by being able to identify even a small bit of it in its native, coevolutionary tongue.

I did, however, almost miss out on learning any of this. The last Dena'ina to speak the dialect of this area died in 1993. It's only because that remarkable man, Peter Kalifornsky, understood the importance of language to culture and committed himself in his last years to preserving it, that I know anything about Dena'ina language. Aside from working out a written language form with a linguist and then writing several books of traditional and personal stories, Kalifornsky also developed language lessons and began to teach again the Dena'ina language to the people who owned it and had lost it — had had it taken from them. The language recovery corresponded to — and surely assisted — a lively cultural revival, even if Dena'ina was listed in the University of Alaska system as a "foreign" language. After Kalifornsky's death, I was able to take a class with an anthropologist, using the books and tapes he left behind.

Even when I don't learn the Dena'ina words, I love to know whatever I can about what they address. To identify mountains, Kalifornsky wrote one word for "ridge broken up into knolls, almost bare," others for "ridge with knolls pointing up," "ridge sloping to a point," "pointed up mountain," "sloping mountain." He listed words for the way trees grow on the mountains: "they grow on the upper mountain slope," "they grow up the mountain in strips," "they grow up the mountainsides," "they grow through the pass." The translations are awkward, but the precisions are clear. Just knowing the richness of words that make up a vocabulary, I look more attentively at mountainsides, see with more exactness their shapes against the sky and the patterns of their vegetation.

There's precision in Dena'ina, and there's poetry, too. The volcanic mountain known as Redoubt I've learned to think of by the translation of its native name — "the one with wrinkled forehead." Kachemak Bay's Sixty-foot Rock has metamorphosed before my eyes, particularly in the warm-weather mirages that are so common, as "soles of feet waving." A distant mountain ridge is rightly known as "ridge where we cry," because from it the Dena'ina who traveled so widely over the land could look down and think about their mothers and fathers and brothers — all their people who went there before them, all their sad and beautiful history, all their connections to one another and to the place that was home. The Roman mythology behind the names of our months surely has its own attractions, but can June, September, and January convey the same passion for living in this land as "king salmon month," the "month leaves turn yellow," the "month we sing?"

※

My experience in discovering a comfortable and comforting fit between a native language and its place of origin surely has repeated itself all through America's history, even as one ancient language after another was eradicated. Thoreau made a point on his trips into the Maine woods of learning the Penobscot and Abenaki names of birds, plants, and places from his Indian guides. He learned that the native name for the fish he knew as "pout" was descriptive of its habit of leading its young as a hen leads her chicks — something he had himself observed but never found in any book. From the Abenaki words for fir branches (*sedi*) and the act of spreading fir branches on the ground for a bed (*sediak*), he understood not only a relationship, but a different way of seeing. When he studied a dictionary of Abenaki language he discovered the very large and nuanced vocabulary used to identify, for example, the types and parts and materials of canoes.

Thoreau wrote in his journal, "It was a new light when my guide gave me Indian names for things for which I had only scientific ones before. In proportion as I understood the language, I saw them from a new point of view. . . . A dictionary of the Indian language reveals another and wholly new life to us."

Later, when Thoreau traveled to Minnesota for his health, he picked up some Dakota vocabulary, including the lovely meaning of the river name, Minnesota — "sky-tinted." The word for waterfall was *ha-ha*, which also meant to curl (as water curls in a waterfall) and to laugh (as the corners of the mouth curl.)

The idea that language shapes the way we see and understand the world was popularized in the 1930s by a linguistic scholar named Benjamin Lee Whorf. The theory, known as linguistic relativity, was put this way by Whorf: "We cut nature up, organize it into concepts, and ascribe significances as we do, largely because we are parties to an agreement to organize it in this way. All observers are not led by the same physical evidence to the same picture of the universe, unless their linguistic backgrounds are similar, or can in some way be calibrated." Every language, Whorf said, has its own pattern-system by which its speakers not only communicate but also analyze nature, notice or neglect certain relationships, and channel reasoning. Without the words or structure to articulate a concept, that concept won't occur. Likewise, if a language is rich in ways to express certain sorts of ideas, then its speakers will habitually think along those linguistic paths. The picture of the universe, Whorf insisted, shifts from tongue to tongue.

Other language experts and cultural anthropologists later discredited much of Whorf's theory — which he sometimes stretched to unprovable and extreme conclusions — but the basic idea of linguistic relativity has never been entirely abandoned.

Much of Whorf's study was of the Hopi language, which he discovered differed rather dramatically from Indo-European languages in concepts of time. Hopi doesn't divide time into rigid past-present-future tenses, but into two modes — objective (the manifest, or things that exist now) and subjective (the unmanifest, things that can be thought about and thus belong to a state of becoming). The Hopi language, thus, has embedded into it an attitude — shared by various other Native American languages and cultures — in which fixed points of time are less important than the "becoming," the process, possibilities, the cyclical nature of time. The language structure reflects and reinforces the cultural values, and thus, the person living in that language understands and responds to the world differently than does the English-speaker who attaches-*ed* to his verbs or places *will* in front of them. The Hopi language developed in a particular place to serve its speakers' particular needs, and the language then helped perpetuate the worldview from which it came.

Where Whorf overstated his case was perhaps both in denying the actual complexity with which the Hopi language deals with various aspects of time, and in making somewhat circular arguments — a person speaks this way and so he must think this way, and so he speaks this way — that are difficult to prove with scientific methods.

Whorf, of course, emerged from a time when many people still believed that "primitive" cultures had rather simple languages that were "undeveloped" compared to those of Europe. He was intent on demonstrating that there were no such things as primitive languages — only different ones with varying emphases. He wrote that "many American Indian and African languages abound in finely wrought, beautifully logical discriminations about causation, action, result, dynamic or energic quality, directness of experience, etc., all matters of the function of thinking, indeed the quintessence of the rational. In this respect they far outdistance the European languages." Among his examples was the Hopi (and many other Native American languages) rendering as verbs many words we know in English as nouns; this system, he argued, was far better suited than English for understanding dynamic states and what we might think of as the science of physics. He pointed as well to the four persons of Algonquian pronouns which allow clear and compact reference to complex social relationships, an African tense distinction between events with and without present results or influences, and, among the Coeur d'Alene Indians of Idaho, the use of three verb forms that discriminate between causal processes — not simply cause and effect, but a more complicated consideration of process.

Similarly, although the Wintu Indians of California disregard verb tense, they tag their verbs with suffixes to specify whether the knowledge they're conveying is known by direct experience or hearsay. Certain Australian languages which appear to lack the words for describing spatial relationships — no "in front of" or "beside" — instead rely on an absolute frame of reference, coordinates that establish the world as one big grid.

Although every person with normal vision sees the same spectrum of colors, the shades are systematized differently in different languages. Some languages, including that of the Dani of New Guinea, identify only two — black and white, or dark and light. Navajo, like Latin, distinguishes between the black of darkness and the black of coal; it has one word for gray and brown, another for blue and green, but includes in its "yellow" category some of what English-speakers think of as green. Experiments have shown that people from cultures with large and precise color vocabularies are better able than those with few color words to pick out colors they were previously shown — that having words by which to know the colors helps a person remember them.

Everyone knows the axiom that Eskimos have hundreds of words for snow. Although this has been overstated — actually, Eskimo languages don't have all that many root words for different kinds of snow but form specialized words by adding to the roots, like adjectives — it is still true that people in northern climates speak of (and thus also see and consider) their ice- and snowbound environments with a keen precision. There are important survival distinctions to be made between a snow that can easily be cut into blocks for shelter and one that will soon turn to rain. Alaska's Aleuts have a word that translates as "the snow that melts the snow," to designate the wet snowfall of spring — that which seems to hasten the melt of the old snow beneath it. (Since I've learned this concept, I've come to think of spring snow with a new appreciation, a more accepting attitude toward winter's end.) In sharp contrast, we find that the Aztec language has just a single word — with different endings — for snow, ice, and cold.

Such richness of linguistic resource can clearly help people address the series of distinctions and subtle gradations they confront from day to day. The Hanunóo people of the Philippine Islands have different names for ninety-two varieties of rice and can easily distinguish differences in rice that would be invisible to the rest of us. Similarly, Alaska's Dena'ina have an entire lexicon with which to describe different kinds of streams, different kinds of trails. It makes a difference if a stream is a river, a tributary, the outlet of a lake, a straight stretch of water, a place of fast or slow current, covered with slush ice or overflow ice. Likewise, a trail is not just a trail; it's a packed snow trail or a trail with snow drifted over it, an animal trail, a snowshoe or sled trail, a trapline trail or a trail used for getting wood.

The same wealth of Dena'ina language applies to salmon and other fish — not only the names of the fish but specialized words to distinguish between dried fish, half-dried fish, a bundle of dried fish, fish dried in one day's wind, fish dried with eggs (roe) inside, fish dried ungutted, fish dried flat, smoked fish, half-smoked fish, the backbone of the fish, the fish belly, the fat, the fatty part just in front of the king salmon's dorsal fin, the roe, dried roe, fermented roe, frozen roe, salted roe, and roe soup. If only I knew all these words, surely I would be that much more involved in the universe of fish and the variety of foods they give us. I wouldn't have to think about how to describe something, because the word would already exist; I would know from the roots of words and their specificity what was important, how one thing related to another.

Along my trail in Dena'ina country, I sometimes try to imagine how differently — or more clearly — I might see my world if I had the Dena'ina language precision with which to know my surroundings and my place in them. I look at a fern and think "fern," but what if the word I thought was *uh t'una*? I would know then with particular clarity that I was seeing and thinking about the leafy part of the plant, in contrast to *uh*, the underground parts of the plant used for food. I might also think *etnen tselts'egha*, literally "ground's coiled rectum," and mean very specifically the fiddlehead portion of the plant. With these words as my own, surely I would connect more strongly to the particular stages of fernhood and their applications to my life, would even find the humor in their associations.

Unfortunately, few of these words are spoken anymore, one person to another in the course of daily living. Of the original five dialects of the Dena'ina Athabascan language, one has been gone a long time, the second is no longer spoken with any fluency since Peter Kalifornsky's death, and perhaps only fifty (mostly elderly) individuals still speak the other three. What remains of the various dialects has been assembled into dictionary form by linguist James Kari, now retired from the University of Alaska's Native Language Center. If not for Kari, Dena'ina words would be scattering silently and irretrievably into the winds.

⁂

Once there were between ten thousand and fifteen thousand separate languages in the world, each evolved in its own place to address the particulars of life in that place. Today there are just six thousand. Up to half of these are no longer being learned by children and will probably become extinct within the next century.

"They are beyond endangerment," says linguist Michael Krauss, a specialist in Alaska Native languages who, like Kari, is now retired from the University of Alaska. "They are the living dead."

Of the three hundred Native languages once spoken in North America, about 210 are still spoken. (About fifty of these are in California, which has been called the world's third most linguistically diverse region, after New Guinea and the Caucasus.) Very few of the 210 are, however, still spoken by children. Even Navajo, by far the largest language group, spoken by some two hundred thousand people, appears to be in trouble. A generation ago, 90 percent of Navajo children entering school spoke Navajo; today exactly the reverse is true — 90 percent of Navajo children entering school speak English but not Navajo. In Alaska, only two of the twenty native languages (Siberian Yupik and Central Yup'ik) are still spoken by children at home and one language — Eyak — lost its last Native speaker in 2007. Krauss believes that *all* Native-American languages, despite bilingual programs in schools, are today threatened.

The roots of Native-American language extinctions lie, of course, with the conquest of Native-American people and the eradication of their cultures. Even after the wars and removals ended and were replaced with assimilation policies, white Americans believed that Natives would be best off abandoning their "inferior" cultures and identities and adopting the "superior," English-only, mainstream American one. Until the 1960s, Alaska Natives were forbidden to speak their own languages in schools, and children were punished for doing so. Parents were told that they were only holding their children back by speaking Native languages at home, and so they too were silenced.

Today's bilingual programs cannot replace the traditional way of learning language, parent to child. Language loss is further exacerbated by the widespread influence of television and "global culture." Perhaps the best that can be done at this late date is to teach Native languages as second or even third languages so that the generations coming along can learn at least some basics of their ancestral languages, enough to maintain respect for them and for their heritages and to continue some ceremonial and artistic uses.

"Preservation," Tlingit oral historians Richard and Nora Marks Dauenhauer have reminded us, is what we do to berries in jam jars and salmon in cans. Preserved foods are different than thriving berry patches and surging runs of salmon, and dictionaries are not the same as speech. Books and recordings can preserve languages, but only people and communities can keep them alive, a vital part of a living tradition.

Meanwhile, fewer and fewer languages dominate; the fifteen largest are spoken by half the world's population. English today is spoken almost everywhere — even though it developed only in a place called England. English, in its youthfulness (only seven hundred years old compared to America's aboriginal languages, which reach back many thousands of years) and with all its borrowings from far-flung and disparate cultures, has little sense-of-place grounding. Indeed, its beauty lives elsewhere, partly in its suitability for addressing commerce and politics; it has a rich and nuanced vocabulary for discussing such things, and a business-like structure. In its domination of the world's discourse, it has succeeded in emphasizing commercial more than natural or spiritual values.

Most thinking people are aware of and concerned about the mass extinction of species we're now facing on this earth because of our interventions in the natural world. We understand the need for species diversity, and thus the imperative to protect what we can. Surely, human languages and the cultures they represent are no less important. Diversity in languages plays the same role as diversity in species; it adds to the web of life in ways we may not even begin to understand.

For a start, we must accept that each language is a worldview — a unique way of organizing the world, with a beauty and complexity all its own — and that any language extinction is a loss to us all, a diminishment of the world. With language extinctions, we lose priceless ways of knowing, exact information, entire concepts. We lose the ability — even the opportunity — to know the world in different ways, to *think* differently.

We can't know right now what it is we may need from the language of California's Pomo Indians, or from the New Guinea Dani or the Gwich'in of Alaska, anymore than we know what we might need from a vine in a South American rain forest or a deep-ocean worm. But we should know that all things have purpose and connect somehow to everything else.

Back at my fish camp, the sky opened, and a hard, dumping rain pounded the metal roof, the alders, the squally inlet. When the rain stopped I walked behind the cabin to pick fireweed shoots for a salad. The air was fragrant with plant oils and wet earth, and all the leaves and grasses were magnified by the droplets caught in their creases and dangling from their tips. A warm white light suffused the breaking clouds; its shafts pierced the mosaic of green and gray inlet waters. There's a Dena'ina word for what I was seeing—that fresh-scrubbed, brightened, new-world look. *Htashtch'ul.* I have a hard time getting my Anglo tongue around this wondrously trippy word, but it's enough for me to know that there is such a word, a single word, to capture what was otherwise so large around me. The English translation — "it is bright after a storm" — stands feeble beside it. The world everywhere after rain looks fresh and lovely, but for me to have a word to put to it — a word that came from this place, that tells me what the first people saw and what significance they gave by naming it — this helps me see with a keen exactness, makes me feel even a little more at home.

Surely, in the Dena'ina part of the world where I walk, the language that is as native to it as its blue-backed salmon and alder thickets deserves to be kept alive for what it contributes to the place and to our understanding about what it means to live purposefully in this place or anywhere.

For any of us, the beginnings of being at home in our places should logically begin with paying attention not just to their natural systems and nonhuman inhabitants but to the ways they were seen and understood by those people who were their first, most adapted and intimately knowing, residents. Native American languages speak to a different relationship to the natural world than Indo-European ones, and if we're indeed to learn to live at home in this land we call America, we would do well to understand at least something of them. As we name, we perceive; as we perceive, we value; and as we value, we honor and protect. Words have power. Languages connected to place can help us respect local knowledge, investigate systems of knowing and seeing, approach nature and culture with a ground-level view. They can help us ask and answer the tough questions about how the human and nonhuman can live together in a tolerant and dignified way. They can help us extend our sense of community, what we hold ourselves responsible for, what we must do to live right and well.

The Dena'ina greeting is *Yaghali du?* "Is it good?" Not, "How are you?" but, "Is it good?" There is, in the question, the assumption that something larger is at stake than the feelings of the two speakers, something less anthropocentric, less egocentric. If it is good, then we shall all — me, you, our community, the larger world — prosper together, not the one individual at the expense of others.

Yaghali du? Yaghali du? The answer we want is *Aa'yaghali.* Yes, it is good. It is all good.

ZEN MOOSE

On an overcast evening in June I was working in my upstairs bathroom, sanding walls for a coat of paint, when I was startled by a tremendous crashing in the alders just outside my opened window. I looked down at a cow moose with two copper-as-new-pennies calves. The cow I recognized, an old girl with a scar on her right shoulder; I'd seen her earlier in the year with a grown calf. Her frolicsome new twins, perhaps two weeks old, now butted under her belly for noisy and energetic suckling. Mama grunted and went on tearing at the alders, grabbing a branch and sliding her mouth down its length so that she stripped it of leaves that ended as a wad against her lips and were promptly tongued in and swallowed.

The three animals, between the dark wall of my house and the row of alders surrounded by grass and fireweed, were shielded from all the world — except for me, peering down like a bird from a nest. I put aside my sanding block and turned off the radio, to watch the leaf stripping, the suckling, one of the calves biting tentatively at the top of some fireweed. The calves now and then bleated like young goats. The cow moaned as they tugged at her, then touched her great gray muzzle to their faces with what seemed, at least to me, like affection.

Ken and I live in a downtown subdivision of a small Alaska town, in a benchland area that was once the reserve of wintering and calving moose and is now populated with streets and houses. It was our conscious choice to not have a mown lawn of imported grass and ornamental shrubs, but to let the yard grow up again the way it was before the foundation hole was dug. Each spring, moose graze the new cow parsnip leaves at the base of the old stalks, and pine siskins flock through the alders and elderberry. At the start of summer, every year, moose calves find their shelter in the shadow of the small house.

It's an irony that, though people increasingly displace moose and their usual sources of food, moose have also found comfort and safety among people. The moose in my yard, despite the threats of cars and free-running dogs, were safer in the heart of a human community than they would be in wilderness. In Denali Park, where bears and wolves are active members of the ecosystem, only 10 to 20 percent of moose calves ordinarily survive their first year. In my town, twin calves routinely grow to maturity.

The greatest obstacle to my urban moose would be finding enough to eat. Alder is definitely not a choice food, but the willow and birch moose favor were being lost to both development and over-browsing. When winters are hard and the lowlands fill with more animals than the browse can support, moose lie down and die of starvation before our eyes. Feeding is not an answer. Every year well-intentioned people put out carrots and bales of hay, but too often the sorry result is habituated, aggressive moose that chase children at their bus stops and separate shoppers from their grocery sacks.

While I fixed and ate dinner in my kitchen, the three moose lay outside my window near eye level. We were only three feet apart, clearly aware of one another, and I thought how odd it was that we all seemed to know that the pane of glass between us was impenetrable, that we inhabited utterly distinct, nonintersecting territories. I looked at the moose, and the moose looked at me — their three sets of eyes all the same size, enormous on the calves, sunken into the old cow's long face.

The cow heaved when she breathed, and looked less than robust. She was still shedding her winter coat, and her fur hung on her in pale, washed-out patches. The bones of her face and all along her back stood out, not from thinness, I thought, so much as age; she reminded me more than anything of an elderly pet mouse, thin-furred and arthritically angular, that I'd had as a child.

Later, in the downstairs room on the opposite side of the house, I stretched out on the couch to watch a video, one of Bill Moyers' *Language of Life* series. Poet Robert Hass was reading haiku he'd translated from ancient Japanese. His words were accompanied by an odd series of whimpering grunts and rumblings. When I opened the blind I found that the three moose had circled the house and were now bedded down in the grass outside this other window. I was about equidistant between them and the television, and was receiving stereophonic sound.

I stopped the video to study the moose again. The downy-furred calves were nearly hidden in the grass, but the cow sat alertly, her head high, ears twitching and turning. In the western light, her heavily-veined, translucent ears looked exactly like darkened cabbage leaves.

I returned to the couch and video. The moose resumed making their noises. I stopped the video. They stopped. I started the video. They started. I realized that the calves, sprawled in the grass, were responding to the sound, the talk, the poet's richly soothing voice. The noises they were making were rhythmic, more than breathing, somewhat like snoring, like purring but not like purring. I had a strange feeling that, from the start, the animals had been drawn to my domestic tones — my radio and sanding, my cooking — and had followed me around the house to settle, purposely, beside the television.

On the video, Hass read a haiku about a full moon and snails crying in a pan, and then he spoke to Moyers about the problem of finding the right word in English to translate what those snails were doing.

While he was saying this, I was listening to the moose calves and trying to name their sound. It was not mooing and not mewing, but it was something like both, and then the correct word came to me. The young moose were mewling.

In his next breath, Hass said that perhaps the best word to describe the sound made by the snails in the pan was *mewling*.

I could only shake my head in amazement. What inexplicable moment was this, that Bill Moyers, Robert Hass, an ancient Japanese poet, and three moose in my yard could engage me in a single conversation? In a salon of my own making, I had met the language of life, exactly.

HONK

IT WAS, AS THEY SAY, a good day for ducks. Or geese. It was also a pretty typical day at the end of the Alaska Peninsula, that treeless edge-of-the-world country graced with three feet of annual precipitation, a mean wind velocity of over sixteen miles per hour, and, on average, a sparse thirteen cloud-free days a year. The hard, shotgun blasts of wind-driven rain had eased off and left biologist Kristine Sowl and me in a steady, soaking drizzle that ran off our head-to-toe waterproof gear as we made our nest in the tall grass at the edge of Izembek Lagoon. On the water before us, between shore and the rain-shrouded barrier islands that separated us from the Bering Sea, thousands of geese paddled and rested and pulled at mouthfuls of stringy greens. This was life at the largest eelgrass bed in the world.

Kristine, in 2001 the sole biologist with the small-by-

Alaska-standards 417,533-acre Izembek National Wildlife Refuge, quietly set up her scope for the "goose count." The object was not exactly to count numbers of Pacific black brant — a job more easily and accurately done by aerial survey in a small plane — but to record the proportion of juvenile to adult birds in order to gauge that year's reproductive success on the birds' breeding grounds to the north. We had hiked to the lagoon's edge a couple of hours before high tide, ready to examine the geese as the rising tide brought them closer to shore and our hiding place.

It was still, in mid-September, early in the brant migration. At present, perhaps fifty thousand brant were staging in the thirty-mile-long lagoon. Soon, though, the numbers of brant would triple to include virtually the entire world's population of the species. For up to eight weeks every fall these birds — arriving from Russia, Canada, and Alaska breeding grounds — use the protected, food-filled waters of Izembek and a smaller lagoon just to the south, Kinzarof, to recover from the stresses of breeding and molting and to fatten up for their long, non-stop migrations to wintering grounds in Mexico. Their leave-taking is usually a mass exodus on the back of a November storm system, although a few thousand normally remain all winter in the ice-free portions of the two lagoons. In spring, brant returning from Mexico stop again at the eelgrass beds to build their fat reserves for breeding.

I settled, cross-legged, into position and dug out a reasonably dry piece of airline napkin to clean my eyeglasses. I was thinking of those black brant facts I'd learned before flying all the way out to Cold Bay and how little my sense of expectation matched the landscape I found myself sitting in. Oh, I'd been to the Alaska Peninsula before, but not to Cold Bay, the town where the refuge had its headquarters and the one inn/bar/store was called the Weathered Inn, or to the north side of the peninsula, with its barrier islands and long views out to what seemed a very lonely Bering Sea. The country — treeless, pressed under a lid of heavy iron clouds, whipped by the unrelenting wind, humming — felt enormous and a little frightening.

As it happened, soon after my arrival in Cold Bay, hijacked planes had been flown into New York's Twin Towers and I'd been awakened in the dark by someone shouting about the end of the world. I'd later spent several hours transfixed and sickened before the refuge headquarters' television as, over and over again, the towers flamed and fell. With every airplane in the country grounded, it was hard not to feel very distant and very isolated, almost as if civilization as we'd known it had come to an end and what was left was ocean, sky, and birds paddling in circles.

I had come to Izembek for a specific purpose: to witness those birds and to consider a controversy that seemed uncompromisable — a desire by some to link Cold Bay and its airport to the larger community of King Cove by road. Such a road would go through or otherwise threaten the refuge, with its brant and other wildlife.

Kristine handed me her waterproof notebook and asked me to write down the numbers she called out. With numerical counters in both her hands, she peered studiously through the scope at the nearest flocks and began clicking with her thumbs — adult birds on one hand, juveniles on the other. When we broke to reposition the scope, she shook her head. "Not good," she said. As in the counts she'd made elsewhere around the lagoon, the numbers of juvenile brant were low: only about one to fifty adult birds. Nesting success that summer in western Alaska had been poor, by all reports; heavy rains and flooding had washed out nests, and predation by foxes had been high. Even before that, the Pacific black brant was considered a species in decline, vulnerable because of its dependence on limited food sources — the geese eat only eelgrass and sea lettuce — and its low tolerance for disturbance.

With my binoculars, I couldn't tell one brant from another, but when I got my turn at the scope, I was surprised at just how well I could see the markings. Juveniles lack the characteristic white neck rings and whitened flanks of the older birds and have instead whiter feathers in their wings. I could clearly see, too, the energetic gobbling of eelgrass, action that reminded me of sucking up strands of spaghetti.

It's those eelgrass beds that lie at the heart of Izembek's habitat significance and have resulted in the lagoon's and refuge's many layers of official recognition — which include both federal and state protections going back to 1959, wilderness status for most of the refuge land in 1980, and international recognition for wetlands values in 1986. The Pacific black brant is not the only waterfowl species to depend on Izembek Lagoon and surrounding lands. Among the flocks that were the objects of our attention intermingled a few Canada geese, larger and with longer necks; maybe fifty thousand of these, mostly the Tavener's subspecies, stage at Izembek in the fall to feed on eelgrass and berries. Large numbers of Emperor geese, perhaps fifty-five thousand — again, most of the world's population — also pass through, feeding on eelgrass in the lagoons and invertebrates and mussels along the beaches. Huge numbers of ducks also concentrate at Izembek in the fall for feeding. Among these, Steller's eiders — a threatened species — are present for most of the year, with half the world's population using the area for molting.

A couple of days before, I'd accompanied refuge staff and other volunteers onto the lagoon in an attempt to herd flocks of flightless molting eiders into a trap for banding. Because the winds and locations of the birds were problematic, the effort was called off for that day, but not before I'd gotten a good look at the western end of the lagoon. The richness of the environment was stunning: the noise of geese that nearly darkened the sky when they flew, dozens of seals hauled out on a bar, sea otters with pups clutched to their chests, a litter of broken crab shell along the shore, most of all the incredibly thick beds of eelgrass — covering most of the shallow lagoon and fouling our boat propellers when we lost the narrow channels that twisted through them.

Eelgrass, a plant that grows in areas of shallow seawater, features very long, flat leaves about the width of audio cassette tape. In fact, the piles of it that wash up dead and brown along the shore look like nothing so much as colossal tangles of old tape. The unique structure of Izembek Lagoon — a basin protected by barrier islands from wind and waves — provides an ideal environment for its growth. The robust yields of good green vegetation provide an energy-packed food for all those waterfowl as well as a rich nursery habitat for fish and invertebrates.

Moreover, Izembek's eelgrass beds are thought to play a major role in the cycling of nutrients into the food web of the Bering Sea. Many thousands of tons of carbon, nitrogen, and phosphorous are produced annually within the lagoon and pass into the waters beyond.

When I'd first arrived at the refuge, manager Rick Poetter had taken me on a drive through some of the refuge lands, their tundra beginning its fade to yellow and rust. He wanted me to get a sense of the geography, the home to terrestrial wildlife including some three hundred brown bears, a caribou herd, several packs of wolves, shorebirds, and songbirds. Dozens of salmon streams wind through the lowlands. At a high point — despite winds that swatted us with horizontal rain and threatened to rip the doors off his truck — we were able to stand on a mountainside and view both the Bering Sea to the north and the Pacific Ocean to the south. At low tide, the lagoon's mudflats and eelgrass beds were exposed, the channels a lighter gray winding through them.

The road we traveled that day, a rough track partially graveled, belonged to a fairly extensive road system within and around the refuge, leftovers from the area's unique history as a World War II military site. Those forty-seven miles of roads, which provide Cold Bay (the town, population seventy) with access to two points on the lagoon as well as to fishing streams and coves on Cold Bay (the bay), lie either outside the refuge or within its non-wilderness 5 percent. The road we took toward Frosty Mountain was an anomaly in that it extended into a wilderness area but was excluded from it by having its corridor narrowly carved out of that protective status. Along the way we viewed old power poles (rubbed and chewed by bears), gravel pits, numerous depressions in the tundra where buildings had once stood, and stunted nonindigenous spruce trees. All are relics of the secret fort that supported twenty thousand troops during the war, when it looked as though the Japanese might work their way across Alaska to try to take North America. The airport in Cold Bay is another of those relics; with the third longest runway in Alaska, it's still well-equipped and designated as an alternative landing site for the space shuttle.

Seeing all that old stuff made one aspect of the road controversy clearer to me. Lands around and even within the refuge are far from pristine, and some folks don't see what the big deal is about running one more road, for local use, between communities. Since at least 1975 residents of King Cove (population 850) have wanted access to the all-weather airport in Cold Bay. King Cove was otherwise accessible only by small aircraft, fishing boat, and infrequent ferry, and bad weather often made travel difficult or impossible. In the 1990s a proposal for a thirty-eight-mile-long road, in part through Izembek's wilderness, pitted King Cove residents and their governmental representatives against environmental groups and others who opposed both the particular threats such a road would bring to the refuge and the precedent of advancing roads into wilderness areas. In a "compromise" secured by Alaska Senator Ted Stevens, Congress paid $37.5 million for road, ferry, airport, and medical improvements to address King Cove's health and safety issues and specified that no part of any of those improvements could enter or pass over any of Izembek's wilderness.

Those who thought the controversy was over were, however, mistaken. Road proponents were quickly back with a proposal for a road that avoided wilderness lands and connected to a hovercraft facility at the head of Cold Bay near Kinzarof Lagoon — itself a sensitive area, with eelgrass critical to overwintering waterfowl when Izembek Lagoon freezes over. Even as I sat in drizzle, surrounded by the honking and croaking and cackling of thousands of geese, government agencies were evaluating the new proposal and a host of alternatives — including the previously rejected road through wilderness.

I could not have foreseen that, six years later, the $37.5 million meant to settle the issue would have been spent mostly on fifteen miles of single-lane gravel road, from King Cove to a point close to Kinzarof, plus a hovercraft to operate between King Cove and Cold Bay and improvements to the medical clinic in King Cove. Neither could I have imagined that Congress would be actively considering a land swap to allow the new road to extend through the wetlands isthmus between the two lagoons — the wilderness area environmentalists call the refuge's "biological heart" — thus completing the surface link between the two towns. The road that had so recently been so emphatically rejected would threaten once again.

Many other Alaskans, of course, live in roadless areas and face unique transportation challenges. As one Cold Bay resident who opposed a connecting road put it to me, "When you make a choice to live in a remote area, that's the choice you make." But then, most other bush communities don't lie so close to major airports. Over the years, King Cove residents sharpened their lobbying skills, arguing that they'd never been consulted before Izembek was designated as wilderness and that they'd never asked for the $37.5 million "compromise." They promised to be good stewards of the land and resources.

I didn't know what lay ahead, but I couldn't really blame the people of King Cove for wanting a road, especially a public one to be paid for with tax dollars. I could hardly expect them to care more about the brant and the eiders that would be disturbed than about their own safety and convenience. But I did expect decision makers, who should consider the ecological and national-interest values at stake — not to mention taxpayer purse strings — to resist.

As Kristine and I hunkered in the grass, gunshots from our east stirred the feeding geese and caused flocks of them to lift from the water, circle noisily, and settle farther off. Just before they'd left, we'd gotten some good counts — one group of two adults and five juveniles, another of two adults with an impressive eight young. I pondered the irony of worrying that geese would be disturbed by passing cars and trucks more than by lethal hunting. I'd asked Poetter, the refuge manager, about that; the answer was that hunting was one of the purposes for which the refuge was created, the hunting season was short, and the brant, although diminishing in numbers, were not yet protected.

Waterfowl hunting was, without question, the main visitor use in the refuge. Even then, because the area is so remote (634 air miles and a then-$734 round-trip ticket from Anchorage), the effort wasn't great. Poetter estimated that there were perhaps five thousand visitor days in the refuge annually, most by local people for fishing and hunting. Non-consumptive activities such as bird watching and photography played a very small part. When I looked in the guest book at headquarters, only a dozen people had signed in for August; these had included relatives visiting refuge personnel, government biologists come to do studies, people passing through on the state ferry, and a single birder.

More gunshots, and more brant departed our area. The tide was high, the rain had ceased for the moment, and Kristine and I packed up. We walked back across a lightly traveled tundra trail lined with the red stalks of dwarf fireweed, crowberry plants with their dark berries, a few blue monkshood flowers, feathery yarrow, and scatters of wild strawberry plants. A honking Canada goose, wings beating into the wind, passed over us.

The day before, along a salmon stream pulsing with discolored chum salmon, I'd followed a bear trail so well traveled that the tundra was ditched into two parallel grooves. To walk in the track, I'd had to proceed with a lumbering, spread-legged, cowboy swagger. Just for that passage, I couldn't help but feel a little like a bear, an animal still in charge of its wild home. The one bear I'd seen, at a distance, stopped to look at me, and then turned aside and went about its own business.

QUIET TIME

CALL ME SCROOGE IF YOU WANT, but I don't care for Christmas. I don't like the megashopping event it's become, the pressure for gaiety, and the manic pace that most people keep. Midwinter, especially in the north, should be a time of rest. All reasonable animals, like bears, know this.

Christmas week Ken and I have made a habit of escaping to dark, quiet places where we don't have to face colored lights, listen to cheery reindeer-nose music, or dress up and stay out late.

For several years we borrowed friends' cabins on the south side of Kachemak Bay. There, after cutting a supply of wood and starting a fire, we lay around with our books and the honey ham Ken's mother always sends. I immersed myself in Chekhov one year, Margaret Atwood the next. We listened to the sea, to the old spruce trees creaking, to the drip of midwinter thaw. During the short daylight hours we gathered pails of blue mussels, row-boated among otters, beach-combed through fresh piles of rose-colored seaweed and winter flotsam. The electricity we'd expected at one cabin had been knocked out by a fallen tree, and after dark we had only candles and flashlights for illumination. I love to read aloud and to be read to, and I got my wish. In another cabin the calendar said 1964, and the most recent magazines were from 1975. We swept up mummified spiders and made minimal home improvements. We slept long and hard.

Then came a cold Christmas, and even boating across the bay seemed too much effort. Instead, we got into our warm car and drove to a lodge with off-season rates less than a quarter of what summer visitors pay.

You'd never find me at a tourist lodge in ordinary circumstances. But I like a bargain, and I liked the fact that, aside from the staff people, the place was just about abandoned. Ken and I took to our little cabin as though it were one more in our line of woodsy retreats. We built a fire in the woodstove, set our kettle on top, and hunkered down with our books and a view of mountains and river. There was a phone, but it didn't ring, and a television, but it could be turned to the wall.

The tourists who throng the central Kenai Peninsula in summer come mainly for the fishing. True, this part of Alaska has its warm-weather attractions, but to me they don't begin to match those of winter.

To begin with, there's the quiet. Footsteps crunch over the snow. A single magpie yak-yaks from along the river.

Then there's the beauty. After a week of below zero temperatures, and with no wind, hoarfrost had thickened over all the trees. Half an inch and more feathered every limb and twig of the birches and aspens. The spruces, too, dressed out in frosty layers, had become fantasy trees more perfect than any *Nutcracker* dream. Though the sunlight never made its way around the mountains to strike the land directly, the low light that lingered all afternoon cast soft pastels among the whites. The peaks above us blazed, and the Kenai River, ever the most gorgeous of turquoises, swept along between ice-rimmed banks, under rising mists. Eagles winged over the river, and moose raised their heads from among the willow browse.

And the cold. I like cold. I like bracing air in my lungs and on my face, and then I like to come indoors to toast before a fire. The lodge's outdoor hot tub was an added attraction; we lounged in clouds of steam under a full moon, and the ends of my hair froze to jangle against my neck like braid fasteners.

The winter so far had cheated us only of snow, and so our cross-country skis and snowshoes remained in the car. Instead, Ken and I went walking. We walked on a trail and read signs that marked summer's twisted stalk and crowberry. We walked beside the river, listening to the swoosh of ice and counting the fishing lures that hung in trees. On the day before Christmas we drove to Kenai Lake and walked the shore on wind-blown, hard-packed snow, where the only other tracks belonged to moose and coyote.

Despite the cold, the lake was open in its center, and mist hung over the water in gray, scumbled scarves. Broken ice, as thin and clear as window glass, lay in piles along the shore, and more hoarfrost clustered on the snow surface like tissue-paper roses. The mountains cut their sharp stenciled edges into pale sky, and then doubled themselves across the ice and still water.

At first the sounds came like distant, throaty barks and echoing howls, eerie and back-tingling. Wolves? The pitch was high and whining, electronic, otherworldly. Ken and I stood and listened. They came again, the cracking and booming of hardening, shifting ice, and more squeaky-cold music bouncing between the mountains.

In places the wind had blown the beach bare, exposing driftwood sculptures and rounded, ice-crusted rocks. Among the wood and rocks we found, too, the heads and carcasses of last summer's sockeye salmon — exquisite now in their dried, darkened forms, like wood carvings. Their jaws stretched open, their eye sockets formed deep hollows, their curved backs wrapped past delicate single rib and vertebral bones held together by stiff-leather skin the color of iron. And all of them lacey with frost.

The world at that moment looked so sterilely white and still, but beneath the lake's ice schooled millions of young salmon. They thrived in clean water on the nutrients left by their dead, spawned-out parents, and they represented — they were, they are — the basic wealth that has for thousands of years supported the surrounding life. The first people prospered here, and homesteaders, commercial fishermen, sport fishermen and tourists, eagles and magpies, the grasses and alders that grow along the shore, the spruce forest.

As the afternoon shadows climbed the mountains and dusk deepened around the lake, Ken in his sweatpants and I in my cap headed back to the road, our car, our little rented cabin. We didn't expect Santa, and we didn't celebrate Christmas. We did, however, remember to be grateful for our gifts and to count among them our life in the north, the grace of a winter day, and salmon.

THE HIDDEN HALF

FROM PORT WELLS, armed with our topographical map, my friends and I began picking out the mountain peaks — Mount Muir, Mount Curtis, Mounts Coville, Emerson, Gilbert, and Gannett, all named for members of the 1899 Harriman Alaska Expedition. The short dark one in the foreground — Mount Doran — was named for the captain of the steamship that carried that expedition along Alaska's coast for two luxurious summer months. They spent one very significant week cruising within Prince William Sound, "coquetting with glaciers," as the trip historian, naturalist John Burroughs, expressed it.

The Harriman group enjoyed a spell of fabulously clear and calm June weather in the sound. We were extremely lucky to find matching weather in August; the guide on our "26 Glaciers" tour, a six-hour boat excursion out of the town of Whittier, told us we'd hit one of only five days all summer when it had been possible to see the mountains.

Up ahead: Point Doran and Doran Strait, two more significant landmarks named for the captain. I felt unreasonably excited — not about the glaciers we were scheduled to see, or the rafts of sea otters we continued to pass, or the seals basking on icebergs, or the chicken lunch being served on the lower level — but about passing a mere point of land. I was, admittedly, something of a Harriman "dreamer" (to again quote Burroughs, who had identified himself as such on that historical journey) and as taken by our points of reference as a celebrity chaser might be touring the neighborhoods of Hollywood stars.

In the long reach of Barry Arm, we faced massive, ice-jumbled Barry Glacier, the glacier that a hundred years earlier had filled the arm nearly to the point we call Doran and that soon after retreated about five miles, to roughly its current position. Our ship swung wide around the point. The navigational chart I referenced showed depths of just one to four fathoms along a curved underwater ridge — Barry Glacier's terminal moraine, the farthest point to which the glacier pushed before retreating.

In the late 1800s, the charts had ended right there at the head of Barry Arm. There, in 1898, the U. S. Army reconnaissance team that named Barry Glacier (after a favorite colonel) went as close as it dared to the glacier described as "formidable" before steaming back to safety. The glacier, then, was dropping ice chunks twenty times the size of the explorers' boat.

The Harriman expedition just a year later met with Barry at a quieter moment, when the glacier's retreat had opened a bit more of a passage, nearly a mile wide — not a great distance given the height of the glacier, the waves falling ice could launch, and the currents to be navigated. As we motored through the widened Doran Strait, I had no trouble imagining that historical moment.

First, the local pilot had handed the ship's wheel to Captain Doran, saying, "I am not going to be responsible for her if she is to be run into every uncharted channel and frog marsh." Doran took the ship to within half-a-mile of the glacier before stopping.

John Muir, the "other John" on the expedition, was an instigator. Like Burroughs, he was an old graybeard, but unlike Burroughs he was an intrepid Alaskan traveler, whose particular interest lay in the country's glaciers; twenty years earlier he'd paddled with Native guides into Alaska's Glacier Bay, where a prominent glacier was given his name. When Harriman asked him, at the front of Barry Glacier, whether he'd seen enough, Muir launched into a dissertation about the trends of the fjord and surrounding country and speculated that through the passage lay more of the same, a "hidden half of the landscape." Perhaps, he suggested, Harriman could have a boat lowered for him, and he could take a look.

Perhaps, Harriman countered, they could run the ship there. Against all advice of the ship's captain and pilot, he ordered the ship, with the 126 family members, scientists, and crew that relied upon it for their lives, to proceed. "I will take the risk," he said. "We will discover a new Northwest Passage."

The Harriman steamship didn't ground on the submerged moraine, swamp in waves from the calving glacier, or run into uncharted obstacles. It *did*, on its return, get caught in a tidal current and nearly smack into the ice-front of Barry Glacier. The Harriman expedition *did* discover, not a Northwest Passage, but a major piece of geography — twelve more miles of spectacular fjord, eleven more dramatic glaciers, a brave new world of mountains and forests and wildflower fields.

I had known this story for years, but I was at last, *in that same place*, knowing it in an entirely new, ground-truth way. From the back deck, I pointed my little camera one way and the other, commemorating my own, belated entry into magnificence.

The Harriman Alaska Expedition, I must note, had not set out to make geographical discoveries. By the end of the nineteenth century, Alaska had been well explored by Russians, Americans, Spaniards, and the English, who'd left their multicultural names all over the maps. Prince William Sound was inhabited then by the native Chugach and Eyak people and, increasingly, by Americans out to make their fortunes in mining, the canned salmon industry, and fur farming. Burroughs commented upon the gold miners in particular: "Alaska is full of such adventurers ransacking the land."

The aims of the Harriman expedition were, instead, threefold. Edward Harriman, head of the Union Pacific Railroad and probably the richest man in America at the time, was intent on spending a relaxed summer vacation with his family. (His son Averell, later to be governor and diplomat, was eight years old.) He also wanted to kill a trophy-size brown bear. And he'd invited along, in order to benefit the world at large, twenty-five of the country's most eminent natural scientists and natural-history writers, as well as several top artists and photographers. His chartered ship, the *George W. Elder*, was largely at the service of the scientists, who could suggest routes and stops and ask for drop-offs and pickups, that they might do their desired collecting and measuring.

It must have been head-spinning to have been along on the Harriman ride, aboard what they came to call, for the combined expertise shared in evening lectures, "a floating university." Harriman's guests included these remarkable personages: C. Hart Merriam, head of the U. S. Biological Survey and chief expedition scientist, in charge of selecting and managing the rest of the scientific party; William Dall, known as Alaska's first scientist and author of the then-definitive text about Alaska; Grove Karl Gilbert, Western explorer and glaciologist; Henry Gannett, chief geographer of the U. S. Geological Survey; Burroughs and Muir; Edward Curtis, photographer who would go on to famously document Native Americans; George Bird Grinnell, founder of the Audubon Society and an ethnographer of Native cultures; Louis Agassiz Fuertes, the bird artist; and landscape painters R. Swain Gifford (illustrator of Theodore Roosevelt's hunting books) and Frederick S. Dellenbaugh (who had been an artist on the Powell expedition down the Colorado River twenty-seven years earlier). Other expedition members, less remembered today, were leaders in the fields of botany, zoology, geology, forestry, mineralogy, and ornithology. Who wouldn't want to be enrolled in *that* university?

Alaska's glaciers were, then as now, sought for their beauty and scientific value. The Harriman group spent a week in Glacier Bay, Muir's stomping grounds of twenty years previous, where they were surprised to discover not only glaciers in rapid retreat but plank walks laid over the glacial till for the comfort of a burgeoning tourist industry. There, the Harriman women took delight in walking beside crevasses, Muir climbed aboard an iceberg, and the photographers swamped their canoe in a wave caused by calving from the face of Muir Glacier. There, too, a zoologist collected ice worms, previously unknown to science, and others in the party measured, mapped, calculated masses, and looked at trees knocked over by glacial surges. The study of glaciers continued in Yakutat Bay to the west, where several more days were spent exploring the area around Malaspina and Hubbard Glaciers.

At its next stop, in Prince William Sound, the expedition reached country that had been far less visited than that to the east and south and had never been scientifically explored. At massive Columbia Glacier, which they named for the university, they left off a party that included Gilbert, the glaciologist, and Curtis, the principal photographer.

Farther to the northwest, on the same day the expedition boldly entered what they would name Harriman Fjord, they also explored another large fjord at the north end of Port Wells. Although that ice-choked fjord was first mentioned in Vancouver's journals a hundred years before, and then was described by the army survey team in 1898, it was left to the Harriman expedition to give it its first scientific look. Continuing the theme they'd begun at Columbia, they named the two large glaciers at the head of what would become College Fjord, Harvard and Yale, the small glacier that connected to Harvard, Radcliffe, the other glaciers on the west side, Smith, Bryn Mawr, Vassar, and Wellesley, and the main glacier on the east side, Amherst. College affiliations were apparently of major interest to the expedition scientists, who reportedly practiced their alma mater cheers in the ship's salon.

It was already evening when the *Elder* turned west and paused at Barry Glacier before charging into new country. In the long days of an Alaskan June, the evening light must have been particularly warm and illuminative, setting whole mountainsides and peaks on fire. Once around the point, Muir described the scene, in a tribute he later wrote to Harriman: "The sail up this majestic fjord in the evening sunshine, picturesquely varied glaciers coming successively to view, sweeping from high snowy foundations and discharging their thundering wave-raising icebergs, was, I think, the most exciting experience of the whole trip."

Burroughs, a more understated observer than Muir, also proclaimed the going, "where no ship had ever before passed" as "one of the most exciting moments of our voyage. . . . Glaciers hung on the steep mountainsides all about us . . . like the stretched skins of huge polar bears."

Our tour boat, part of the regular but not extensive traffic that enters Harriman Fjord these days, carried us under afternoon sunshine into that same dramatic landscape. The glaciers did indeed — with their great wrinkled backs — look something like Bunyanesque white bear skins. The mountains, unnamed except for those few peaks commemorating Harriman expeditioners, were steep and rugged, the bowls filled with year-round snow and streaked with slides. Mount Muir's serrated top looked fresh-cut against the sky. Even without thundering ice falls, the scene felt primordial, as though we were present at the creation. We were, almost literally, back in the ice-age; these glaciers were among few in the world still very close to their maximum positions of recent centuries, though now rapidly thinning as a result of global warming.

The Harriman expedition ship spent only a few hours within the new fjord, but when it turned back to repair a damaged propeller (a blade broken on ice in College Fjord) and retrieve scientists left at other locations, Muir and the geographer Gannett stayed behind with a small party. As recorded in Muir's journal, this group seemingly made the most of the next three days. Starting from "a paradise of a camp on a bench covered with Cassiope [heather]," they spent "a grand exhilarating evening, pitying them on the ship." The next day, exploring the shore on foot, Muir took note of the glaciers, rock, waterfalls, birdlife (abundant ptarmigan), and especially the vegetation. The group found tree stumps cut by earlier visitors, one of which, a hemlock nine inches across, Muir aged at 325 years old by counting its growth rings. This told them that trees in the region were very slow-growing, and that the areas of old-growth had not been glaciated for at least hundreds of years. The following day they rowed seven miles in rain toward the fjord's mouth and established another camp, near a spot they deduced had been a recent hunting camp and site of a bear kill. The Harriman expeditioners may have been the first people to enter the fjord by ship, but local people had apparently been hunting within it for some time.

I'm fascinated by every bit of this, even the part about rowing and camping in rain, wishing I could propel myself backward in time and sit around a smoky campfire with John Muir and his pals. Another part of my brain marvels at the adventure and hardiness of those scientists who ran up and down mountains with their surveying gear. I know they were frustrated at times, having too little time and so much coastline to cruise. The wishes of the individual scientists to see or study specific locales or phenomena had to be balanced with the Harriman family's touristic impulses and Harriman's drive to shoot a bear, a goal that met with surprising difficulty. Muir was disappointed when the ship bypassed another bay of glaciers that had been scheduled, Harriman having declared that there was no more "ice time." Certainly others felt the same way every time the ship's whistle called them back from their work. Ultimately the expedition's science could amount to no more than a survey or reconnaissance, a sampling of what could be seen and collected at those points along the Alaska coast where weather, time, and terrain allowed.

In 1899, though, even such a limited reconnaissance had its value. The expedition returned with, among other things, five thousand mounted insect specimens and an equal number of professional landscape photographs. From the biological collections, several hundred new species and over fifty new genera were identified, along with their geographical distributions; the collections of marine specimens were particularly strong. Although not a major focus of the expedition, Native cultures were documented and their songs and languages recorded on Harriman's newfangled wax cylinder graphophone. For twelve years after the expedition, teams of additional scientists labored under the direction of lead scientist Merriam on the thirteen volumes of reports financed, like the trip itself, entirely by Harriman. Many of these volumes became standard reference works for later researchers.

It may be that the most significant scientific work of the Harriman expedition was its contributions to glaciology. A history of the expedition written in 1982, *Looking Far North*, called the glacier volume of the expedition's report "the most profound" in the series and its author, Gilbert, "unquestioningly the most brilliant 'scientific' aboard the *George W. Elder* . . . his study of Alaskan glaciers represents the pinnacle of the expedition's contribution to science."

Modern glaciologists do indeed give high marks to Gilbert's glacier study. Retired U. S. Glaciological Survey scientists Mark F. Meier and Austin Post, who studied the glaciers of Prince William Sound for fifty years, described Gilbert's early work as prophetic, his arguments parallel to modern theory. In a report they coauthored in 1979, assessing Gilbert's study of Alaska's tidewater glaciers, they wrote, "Examining Gilbert's documents, the modern glaciologist may be surprised to discover that so many ideas, thought to be new, were in fact anticipated 80 years ago by one of America's most remarkable and brilliant scientists." Although the physical principles Gilbert relied on would today be considered naive, and his arguments were couched largely in descriptive terms, concepts he put forward are extremely similar to what would emerge much later in more defined scientific terms. The questions he raised about glacial calving, erosion, and behavior on the seabed remain prominent in glaciological thought today.

Instead of focusing on theory, as earlier geologists had, Gilbert took a "classical" approach based on observations of behavior, and the behavior he observed he linked to his earlier work in hydrology. Glaciers, he saw, flowed according to many of the same principles as water or molten rock. Moreover he noted that some of Alaska's glaciers were advancing while others were retreating, and he linked these cyclic movements and their rates to climate changes plus local conditions, including topography. He came very close to understanding the major factor controlling the behavior of tidewater glaciers — the depth of water at their termini, which determines how much ice is exposed to the melting effects of sea water. When glaciers push up terminal moraines in front of them, they have less exposure and will melt less; once they melt away from moraines, they have more exposure, will melt more, and typically begin irreversible retreats.

A major value of Gilbert's report certainly lies in its descriptions. On the Harriman expedition, Gilbert studied and described nearly forty glaciers. He made almost that many shore landings, three of which lasted for several days and involved steep climbs to gain the best vantage points. He was able, working with the photographers, the mapmaker Gannett, and others, to document not only individual glaciers and their processes but a landscape marked by hanging valleys, moraines, kettle ponds, and other evidence of previous glacial coverage. He described at length appearances, distances, heights, and even minute details of glaciers and their surroundings. His intent was to build a body of data and observations of very localized areas, that it might be useful to later scientists.

The map made for Gilbert's report of Port Wells, showing Harriman and College Fjords and their glaciers, is amazingly detailed. It drew upon Gannett's surveying with a plane-table, photographs, and the work of previous travelers, and looks, for its bird's-eye accuracy, like something that could only have been produced after the introduction of aircraft.

As part of his commitment to documentation, Gilbert was perhaps the first geologist to recognize the importance of establishing photographic stations that might be returned to year after year as a way of documenting the movement of glaciers and other changes in them and to their surroundings. Several still-in-use stations in Prince William Sound, marked by rock cairns, were first occupied by members of the Harriman expedition, and thus provide a more-than-hundred-year record, something like extreme time-lapse photography. The value of this to scientists is immense, particularly for tracking the advances and retreats of tidewater glaciers, several of which have made dramatic movements over the last century. By comparing the front of Columbia Glacier with the expedition's photographs, later researchers were able to document advances that culminated in 1910, 1921, and 1935. In 1974 hydrologist Post witnessed a small advance, in which ice pushed debris directly over one of Gilbert's stations. Columbia began a drastic retreat in the early 1980s, and today more than ten miles of water separate it from that station.

In Harriman Fjord, our tour boat turned up Surprise Inlet, heading for Surprise Glacier. Surprise — named by the Harriman expedition because, as the first glacier they faced on entering the fjord, it was indeed a "surprise" — is today the fjord's most active glacier and the one the tour boats spend the most time visiting.

When the boat stopped a quarter-mile from the glacier and the door to the front deck opened, I swarmed forward with the rest of the camera-toting tourists. The ice wall, a couple of hundred feet high, was broken into blocks and columns, blue and bluer into its caverns. Behind it, the dirt-streaked ice wound down from rocky, waterfall-coursed, snow-topped mountains. The ice creaked and cracked, much more loudly than I'd expected, and I suddenly understood why the early Spanish explorer Fidalgo could have mistaken, in thick fog, the cracking and booming of Columbia Glacier for the eruptions of a volcano. Small icefalls spilled from Surprise, but those who awaited the kind of calving action that would rock us with waves were disappointed. Floating glacier ice — the smallish kinds known as brash and growlers, as opposed to the larger bergy bits and icebergs — surrounded us. The boat's crew scooped some for our examination and drinks.

"What about Harriman Glacier?" I asked. "Are we going closer?" Far at the fjord's end, that massive glacier was beyond our sight.

The guide looked apologetic. "We'll only view it from a distance."

"Does the boat ever go up to the end?"

"Not very often. Frankly," she said, "Harriman is a boring glacier."

She meant that, as one of the few stable or perhaps advancing glaciers in the sound, Harriman was not as "active" as some of the others, was not calving in dramatic, boat-rocking fashion. Despite its size, it would not be a tourist's delight.

For the moment, though, I was happy to be surprised by Surprise, that gorgeously convoluted, breathtakingly blue, huge and ancient river of ice. After so many years living in Alaska, I sometimes feared I'd hardened to natural beauty, forgetting to be astonished at the landscape I lived within. On this day, if I was not a typical tourist, come from afar to ogle scenery, and if I knew more than what might be entertaining about history, and glaciers, and climate change linked to the retreat of Harriman Glacier in the following years, I would still want to take John Muir's hand in mine and rejoice with the world as it is.

HOW TO BEAR WITNESS

FIRST, HAVE A FRIEND WHO'S CRAZY for bears. Let him invite you, on a morning early in May, to visit the dens of sleeping bears not far from where you both live, on Alaska's Kenai Peninsula. This is something he does every morning through several spring weeks, as other people might take a walk to the post office. Let the particular morning be one in which, a few hours earlier, a 5.4 earthquake shook you from your beds. Know this fact: earthquakes rouse hibernators.

Let your friend know precisely where the bears are sleeping. This he will know because the two females, in separate dens, are each wearing radio collars. Your friend has flown over them in a plane, and the *beep-beep-beep* has pinpointed their locations. Your friend knows what can't be seen — in one den a sow and three yearling cubs, in the other a sow and, presumably, new cubs born during the winter. These are brown bears — the big kind — what in the interior, where they're smaller, people call grizzlies.

Last year your friend kept watch on one of these same bears. He missed one day, and the next he found only tracks, straight out of the den and up over the mountain.

The morning you accompany your friend, ski along the edge of a canyon, through mostly open country, past scattered spruce trees and the top, bowed branches of alders still buried in six feet of snow. Let sun break through the clouds, distant mountains glow, and the *who-who* of a courting snipe float across the land. Let your skis clatter over the frozen tracks of moose and coyote. Your friend will point out the site of an old black bear den and a slope down which he'd once seen a pack of wolves run, and then, across the canyon, a spindly spruce between birches, that marks the site of the first den. There will be no opening, no trail, no evidence that anything has stirred.

Farther along, as you approach the second den, let there be tracks — big ones — on the valley floor. Allow yourself to feel excited. But let the den site itself, that patch of snow-covered hillside your friend points to, right next to a trail where snowmobilers ran all winter, be undisturbed. When you ski down to study the tracks, decide they were made by moose and melted by the sun into huge, pizza-pan-size circles.

Before you leave, ski an extra loop through the high country, following the flight of a snowy owl. Ski with your friend from tree to tree and track to track. Stop to watch ravens and a soaring eagle. Talk about what bears do once they wake and how to tell females from males by their coloring and behavior and what someone said about a bear being killed near Fritz Creek a few days before, "in defense of life and property." Talk about how broadly "in defense of life and property" is interpreted, and that people leave garbage and dog food and horse feed where they'll attract bears and cause their deaths. Say that bears need a lot of space. Know this number: the home range of a female brown bear on the Kenai Peninsula is 160 square miles. Know these other numbers: between 250 and 300 brown bears live on the Kenai.

Calculate this: perhaps 3 percent of all the brown bears on the Kenai are present in the two dens at which you've just looked.

Don't be disappointed that you didn't see bears. Know they're safe in their drowsy nests. Be aware that what your friend does, in his daily attendance at the bear dens, is not only, or primarily, about watching for bears. Witness what is this day in bear country — softening snow, moose browse, the call of a ptarmigan. Be present where bears live, and by your presence testify to the necessity of places that are filled not with people and property but with undivided, left-to-run-wild space and all else that prospers there. Be grateful for the possibility that, sometime in your life, you may have the good luck to find spring bears just out of a den, rolling and sliding and cuffing one another, squinting into a new year's sun. May you see them being bears, and may they not see you.

REPORT FROM THE ROOKERIES

ON THE LAST DAY of my July 2000 seafaring excursion over and around Gulf of Alaska waters, I stepped into the living room of my B&B in the town of Seward and found myself with the objects of my desire, Steller sea lions. The picture on the television was of a sunny rock slope emerging from blue sea, with sea lions both at rest on the rookery and swimming through the swells at its edge. A cacophony of roars and bleating rose amid a clattering of gulls.

The cable feed was coming to us from the Alaska SeaLife Center, a research and education facility down the road. The center was getting its picture by microwave from an island rookery about twenty-five miles out to sea. There a new technology using remote cameras allowed constant monitoring and close observation by researchers hoping to learn something about the lives of Steller sea lions, to shed light on the big questions: why had the western population dropped so dramatically, and what would help it recover? I watched as someone at the center manipulated the camera to zoom in on one of the old bulls, a huge couch-shaped creature with various battle scars across its back, and then to a pile of shiny dark pups, just weeks old. The camera focused on a pup's white flipper tag, number 978. The picture was so sharp it was possible to see even the flies buzzing around the animals.

The day before, I'd taken a tour boat for a ten-hour wildlife cruise out of Resurrection Bay and into the gulf and fjords to the west. Although the advertised route passed Chiswell Island, the rookery I was now seeing on television, this summer the captain had altered his route to avoid any possible disturbance to the 150 or so sea lions, mostly females with new pups, whose summer home it was. Major rookeries were protected by a three-mile exclusionary zone, but Chiswell, which once had rocked with more than a thousand sea lions, was not one of these. By law, boats only needed to keep a hundred yards away.

The reduced Chiswell exemplified, however, what was at stake. Since the late 1970s Steller populations had been in precipitous decline. In 1990 the Steller was listed as threatened under the federal Endangered Species Act, and in 1997 its western stock — from Prince William Sound west through the Aleutian Islands — was downgraded to endangered. Many rookeries had been abandoned altogether, and biologists warned that, unless the decline was reversed, the western stock could be extinct in sixty-five to a hundred years.

On our tour, instead of visiting the rookery, we stopped by a nearby site where a few dozen nonbreeding (juvenile and non-dominant male) sea lions were hauled out. As we drifted slowly between islands we got a good view, with binoculars, of their doglike heads and flower-petal ears, their Rubenesque curves and fleshy folds, the rubbery flippers they waved as they stretched. Wet, the animals were sleek and dark; dry, they blended into the sand-colored ledges on which they lay. Most days, our captain told us, most of the animals spent most of their time lounging. Nights were when they focused on feeding. "Opportunistic feeders," sea lions will eat salmon, flatfish, herring, octopus, cod, pollock — whatever they can catch. As we watched, one largish male — maybe eight or nine

Report from the Rookeries | 83

feet long, more than half a ton of muscle and fat — swam parallel to the boat. He seemed to glide effortlessly through the clear water, like a gleam of light.

We were enjoying, in our captain's words, an "abundance of abundance." From the moment we'd left the harbor we'd seen — one after another and generally in profusion — bald eagles, sea otters, harbor seals, both tufted and horned puffins, Dall's porpoises that played around the boat, murres and cormorants, shearwaters generally seen farther offshore, parakeet auklets, two kinds of murrelets, pigeon guillemots, the first salmon sharks I'd ever seen, the sea lions, numerous pairings of cow and calf humpback whales, one small pod of feeding killer whales or orcas, and one "superpod." Silver salmon were jumping, flocks of kittiwakes fluttered over schools of small fish, the water mixed its planktonic soup. Life was good for Alaska's marine creatures, feeding and fattening on summer bounty.

The high point of the day had to be lingering with that "superpod" of killer whales. Just once a year several family groupings come together to socialize and breed, and we had hit the day. Fifty whales with towering black fins circled and rolled and rubbed up against one another, and we floated beside them with a hundred cameras clicking. These were recognized members of several "resident" pods — fish eaters — not to be confused with the scarcer and stealthy "transient" killer whales that feed on marine mammals.

We witnessed, too, numerous humpback whales blowing and diving, breaching and slapping their long pectoral flippers and their flukes. One calf, as though throwing a tantrum, leapt from beside its mother, again and again, a dozen times launching into the air and falling back with a thunderous splash.

It's natural, I know, for humans to be drawn to the size and drama and responsiveness of whales, and our group — consisting mostly of visitors from outside Alaska — was no exception. The sea otter, too, is a charismatic species; our wildlife watchers had been thrilled with the little groups of whisker-faced, back-lolling, fur-fluffing luminaries we'd paused beside.

Lo, the poor pinnipeds, I thought. There's something pedestrian about seals and sea lions — what we perhaps see as a lumpishness or loutishness, or the lack of excitement as they doze — that fails to endear them to humans. On the other hand, the plainness of Stellers had historically worked to their advantage. Unlike sea otters and fur seals, which had been so valued for the luxuriance of their pelts, sea lions had never been hunted to the brink. They had, instead, been considered as pests and competitors by fishermen and even government agencies, and between 1963 and 1972 — as late as *that* — forty-five thousand Steller sea lion pups were killed under government contracts. Until 1990 fishermen were allowed to shoot sea lions that threatened their gear or catch. And, with the rise of industrialized trawl fishing, many sea lions were accidentally caught in the ships' huge nets. Between 1960 and 1990 perhaps eighty-four thousand western-population Stellers drowned or were intentionally killed in trawl fisheries. Stricter regulation, improvements in technology, and avoidance efforts eventually reduced the accidental catch in fisheries to perhaps a few dozen Stellers per year; of course, by that time, there were many fewer Stellers to be caught.

It wasn't overhunting, eradication efforts, direct fishery conflicts, predation, disease, or pollution that sent the western Stellers into their population dive — although some or all of those factors likely contributed. By 2000, when Alaska's western population was estimated at twenty-five thousand animals, scientists generally agreed that the principal cause of the decline was "nutritional stress." Adult animals were healthy enough, and young animals did fine while they were nursing, but juvenile sea lions between ages one and four weren't surviving. (In 1978 juveniles made up 20 percent of the population; in 1994 they were only 5 percent.) The accepted theory was that the young animals — inexpert feeders that don't dive as deep as adults and can't eat food as large as adults can — weren't getting enough to eat, particularly in winter when prey was scarcest.

What the scientists didn't agree upon was whether the food shortage was a result of fishery effects on food availability, long-term ecosystem shifts that affected food availability, or some mix of the two.

Just the week before my trip by state ferry and tour boat through the heart of sea lion habitat in the Gulf of Alaska, a Seattle judge had responded to a lawsuit by environmental groups by closing all trawling for groundfish (mostly pollock, cod, and Atka mackerel) within all Steller sea lion critical habitat areas. The 121,350 square miles of critical habitat, which surround rookeries and major haul-outs and include three at-sea foraging areas, pretty much blanketed all nearshore waters through south-central Alaska and along the Aleutian Islands. Those areas, altogether the size of New Mexico, had been designated as "critical" to successful sea lion feeding. They were the same areas where fishing effort was increasingly concentrated, where most of Alaska's enormous pollock catch was taken. Researchers had found that the fishery might have been removing 40 percent of the pollock available to Stellers.

The National Marine Fisheries Service (NMFS), the agency responsible both for making sure that groundfish fisheries were sustainable and economically viable *and* for protecting sea lions, for many years rejected the idea that fisheries were harming sea lions. Each time quotas for the fishing fleet were raised, NMFS found the fisheries "not likely" to jeopardize the Steller sea lion. Not until 1998, after being sued by environmentalists, did NMFS formally find that the pollock fisheries in the Bering Sea and Gulf of Alaska were adversely affecting sea lion critical habitat and jeopardizing the stock's continued existence. The agency then reported, "Essentially, the problem is not the total amount of pollock harvested from Alaska water, rather the disproportionate amount harvested from critical habitat and the resultant potential for localized depletion." Regulators subsequently modified the fishery to spread it across time and space.

The recent judge's ruling had slammed the agency for an inadequate response and required that fisheries take place only in areas outside critical habitat — generally farther from shore, away from the richest grounds and those both safest and most economical to fish. Fishermen, fishing companies, and politicians were all in an uproar, cursing environmentalists and the Endangered Species Act.

Earlier, my ferry trip had taken me from Homer, on the end of the Kenai Peninsula, to the fishing-dependent island of Kodiak. Except for the waters very close to Homer, my entire route, to Kodiak and back north to Seward, lay within sea lion critical habitat. Just after leaving Homer, I'd stood on the windswept foredeck with a man from Minnesota who was nearly in a swoon about the sea otters we passed. Never mind that we were moving at fifteen knots and that the otter we got the best look at would have been run over had it not dived at the last minute. "These are the first otters I've ever seen in the wild!" the man exclaimed to me. When I asked him what the highlights of his summer-long Alaska visit were, he said again, "I'm pretty excited about the otters." He gestured with both arms. "Isn't it wonderful that we still have this place left?"

I thought, what if we'd lost the sea otter, as we came so close to doing a century ago? Even two decades ago, otters were rare in the waters we were plying. They've come back under protective law; we still have this place, still have — for now — a living ocean, and sea lions.

Up on the bridge, the ferry's captain told me that the state ferries were attracting increasing numbers of "adventure-type tourists," many of them intent on sighting rare bird species. "We're not a tour boat," the captain said, "but we try to give passengers, not what they want necessarily, but *something*." Sure enough, not long after our visit, the mate announced over the speaker, "Attention, whale watchers," and pointed out a line of blowing humpbacks to starboard. We didn't slow or change course, but we did keep company with the whales, or they with us, for a long time. A little while later the mate announced another humpback that was slapping its tail. It slapped dozens of times, throwing up great crests of white water, and it waved its flippers. We eventually passed just yards from it, as it rolled on the surface and showed us its broad back. The passengers, standing in the big, front observation-room windows or rushing from one outer deck to another, were ecstatic.

We saw harbor seals near Homer, but we didn't spot any sea lions until we reached Kodiak, where several dozen, none too shy, had taken up residence in and around the port. I watched a few swim casually

Report from the Rookeries | 87

by — past the ferry dock, beside a seine boat heading out, along the breakwater, not far from a pair of zooming jet-skiers. I'd heard these animals compared to bears that frequent dumps; they'd been drawn to easy meals that, in their case, come from the fish waste of boats and processing plants.

On the ferry, when I asked the captain what changes he'd seen in his twenty-five years on the same route, he offered that the biggest one was the reduction in sea lions around the Barren Islands, which we'd passed during the night. "In the old days they'd be planing through the water there, hundreds of them. Of course, you don't notice a reduction while it's happening, just as we don't see Columbia Glacier receding, not from trip to trip. But we never see sea lions anymore." He showed me his charts, with the three major rookeries along our course surrounded by bright yellow circles, hand-colored. These were the zones boats had to avoid, and he'd needed to alter the ferry route past two of them.

Later, just north of Kodiak, I went out on the foredeck to watch our approach to Marmot Island, one of those marked-off rookeries — once the largest in the world. (In 1979 6,741 pups were counted there, compared, more recently, to just hundreds.) From a distance, Marmot looked like a giant hatbox, with vertical cliffs for sides and a flat green top. We were too far away to make out the lower rock slopes where the sea lions gathered, and — though the animals are known to forage for many miles out — there were none to be seen in the choppy water. Passengers — including one young man who worked on a trawler — told me they never saw any sea lions except in and around the Kodiak harbor.

During our seven-hour stop in Kodiak, I went to see a biologist who has been, since 1981, involved in assessing marine mammal populations and their interactions with commercial fisheries. As a professor with the University of Alaska's Sea Grant Marine Advisory Program, Kate Wynne had regularly appeared before management panels and congressional committees to urge more research into the Steller issue and to argue against taking precipitous actions such as shutting down fisheries.

Wynne accepted that the Steller problem was one of food, but she wasn't so sure that the fisheries as conducted before the judicial closure were necessarily the problem. "We don't have data . . . adequate to make these decisions," she told me, obviously frustrated, like many in fishing communities, at facing economic costs without any surety that something would be gained. It was true that the phenomenal growth in Alaska's groundfish fisheries corresponded in time and area with the sea lion decline. (A chart circulated by conservation groups showed, between 1977 and 1994, pollock catch in the Bering Sea quadrupling while Stellers were falling to one-quarter of their starting numbers; as a graphic, it formed a neat x.) But it was also, true, Wynne pointed out, that there were other things besides commercial fishing going on in the Bering Sea and Gulf of Alaska. "Ocean conditions are just very different," she said, compared to the 1970s, when there might have been two hundred thousand Stellers swimming those waters.

Indeed, scientists agreed that, as a result of either naturally occurring conditions or a combination of natural cycles and human causes leading to a broader global warming, a North Pacific "regime shift" began in the late 1970s. Water temperatures rose by three to four degrees Fahrenheit, and the warmer water affected the ecosystem in various, still poorly understood ways that favored some species over others and changed predator-prey relationships and the carrying capacity of the ocean. Fatty forage fish like capelin and herring — known to be preferred by Stellers — had become scarce, while the leaner pollock and cod grew to dominate.

At the same time, seabird populations suffered large die-offs, crab and shrimp populations crashed, unusual algae bloomed, sea ice shrunk, and gray whales washed up dead. Populations of pinnipeds other than Stellers — walrus and several species of seals — also declined. Numbers of sharks exploded; most notably, salmon sharks, which thrive on pollock, were said to have replaced sea lions and other marine mammals as the top predators in the Gulf of Alaska.

Wynne, like everyone else, wanted to know why the Stellers had declined so dramatically. And like others, she was wondering if that question might be unanswerable. Researchers were switching their attention to the question the courts said must be addressed — regardless of the *cause* of the decline, what did the Stellers need to *recover*? Ocean temperatures aren't something humans can easily influence, but fisheries fall directly within our control. What effect were the groundfish fisheries having on the Stellers, their food supply, and their habitat?

At the height of that summer, though, Wynne wasn't sure that more pollock for the sea lions was necessarily going to help. One recently published line of research held that an all-pollock diet was a poor one for sea lions, and it noted that the sharpest declines in Stellers had been in areas with the lowest diversity of diet and particularly where diet was dominated by pollock. Studies of captive sea lions fed alternative diets of pollock and herring had shown that all-pollock diets resulted in significantly lower energy intakes.

"It isn't just fishermen versus sea lions, with fish in the middle," Wynne said to me, gesturing past her window. "I look out here and see a whole lot of predators — birds, seals, fish, whales, people. You need to look at the whole system. Look at the fish that eat the fish." A possibility that concerned Wynne was that, by not removing large pollock — the target of the trawl fishery — from the critical habitat areas, those large, notoriously cannibalistic fish could decimate the smaller-sized pollock that juvenile sea lions depend upon. Another possibility was that less pollock fishing (less removal from the "niche" that pollock now fill with such dominance) would slow the cyclical return to a regime populated by other, fattier fish — the varied diet that could most benefit sea lions in the long run. These hypotheses had not been tested; indeed, it would be difficult to design, in a dynamic environment, the research to do that.

In considering the range of predator-prey relationships, Wynne also didn't discount killer whale predation as at least a factor in holding down the Steller population. In the Aleutians, killer whales that had formerly depended on sea lions had been observed shifting their predation to sea otters, and in just a few years the otter population had plummeted by 70 percent.

Meanwhile, sea lion research — driven by the court battles and the fishing revenues at stake — continued. Wynne did one piece of it, spending many of her days in a lab picking through sea-lion scat to see what was being eaten. At the SeaLife Center in Seward, an ongoing study involved feeding captive sea lions a series of diets corresponding to what sea lions ate in the Gulf of Alaska before the decline, in the gulf after the decline, and in southeastern Alaska where there'd been no decline. The primary researcher on that study offered me his opinion that an all-pollock diet was probably not the most nutritious for sea lions but that to conclude that it was a bad diet "is like saying that vegetables aren't good for people."

I came from a fishing town myself and was sympathetic to fishermen — especially those who worked the smaller boats close to home, as opposed to the huge factory ships that sailed out of Seattle. I was sorry to see fishermen and environmentalists on opposing sides, distrustful of one another. We all want easy answers, as easy as the old sea-otter solution had been. Stop killing them, and they'll come back. But nothing in the ocean or in our complex economic and management systems is so simple anymore.

In the Kodiak harbor, the salmon seine fleet was loading supplies and heading out for an opening the next day, and schools of salmon smolt darkened the water. I stopped to talk with a halibut long-liner who was, with his family, cleaning his boat and putting away gear. He was not a fan of the trawlers. "I want everything to be healthy," he said. "Just because some oddball thing like a bryozoan grows on the bottom doesn't mean it's not valuable in the environment. Reasonable fishermen have to be ecologically sensitive. The health of the habitat is critical to us."

While he supported the recent court decision, he was made nervous by it, fearful that it would lead to other fishery closures. "I understand the people who live in San Francisco or Omaha want to protect the whales and sea lions. That's good. My fear is that environmental groups will become radicalized in order to get anything done."

Any of us, I agreed, would prefer to take care of our own homes, rather than have outsiders with simplistic understandings, a sometimes overdose of emotion, and blunt tools like lawsuits telling us how to live.

Before leaving town I stopped in at the new Alutiiq Museum, which preserves and shares the culture of the original people of the region. As I circled through I was impressed again and again by what a marine-oriented life these people had led — indeed, still led. The fishing nets woven from porpoise sinew, the ivory harpoon points, the sealskin boots, the baleen baskets, the fur parka decorated with puffin beaks — nearly everything in the physical culture was used to wrest a living from the sea, was a product of the sea, or both. Sea lions, aside from being an important source of meat and oil, supplied the hides needed to cover Alutiiq kayaks. Their long whiskers adorned hunters' hats. Local people didn't live quite that way anymore, although the arts of traditional kayak building and hat making were still vitally alive, and Natives throughout Alaska still hunted sea lions — some five hundred each year — for subsistence purposes. And Kodiak, despite constant change, was still an island whose people lived with the sea and what it provided. I understood their fears about losing livelihoods based on fishing, and I thought that most of them understood that sustainable resource use in the long run was as essential to their community as it was to the rest of the marine ecosystem.

Meanwhile, there was some good news from the field. A survey of eleven major rookeries, including the three I passed on my ferry trip, found roughly the same number of pups as the last survey, two years before. Biologists also found more capelin and other oily forage fish within the critical habitat areas, amid signs that the natural cycle might be swinging back to a regime more suited to such fish. Researchers, guardedly optimistic, suggested that the sea lion decline might be bottoming out.

The years to come, with intensive research, would begin to unlock some of the sea lion's mysteries while revealing new ones. Our species, with its magnificent brain power, was poised to expand its understanding of ecosystem dynamics that were enormously complex in all their relational parameters. What we would do with that learning was still to be seen, but as I took a last walk back to the ferry dock I was stuck on a singular thought: an animal that had survived natural cycles in North Pacific waters for three million years deserved a whole lot more than a wave good-bye.

THE FARTHEST ISLAND

I.

The island emerges, finally, from fog. I'm thinking of the old days, when ship captains plunging through fog could only locate land from the sounds of waves breaking on shore and seabirds crying from their rookeries. As our anchor chain rumbles out, I stand at the rail with passengers, watching the darkness that is the island rise into low and wooly clouds.

A passenger says to me, "You must get to visit these amazing places all the time." He says this because he knows I live in Alaska, and because he does not really understand where we are.

I say, "Well, actually, I've been to the Bering Sea a few times now, but this is only the second time I've been lucky enough to come *here*. This place is as far from anywhere that you'll ever be."

I'm the historian on the cruise ship staff, but St. Matthew Island is thin on human history. I'm fond of imagining the members of the Harriman Expedition landing here in 1899 to collect newly discovered buntings they called "hyperborean snowflakes." I know little more of their visit than that they explored the remains of a driftwood shelter while William Dall told them the story of three Russian fur hunters who shipwrecked on the island many years before.

I share this story with those on deck. A rescue ship that came looking for the hunters the summer after their disappearance found just one survivor on the island. That man told his rescuers that the other two had floated off on ice floes. "Unlikely," I say to those around me. "Everyone assumed he'd eaten them."

The passengers step away from me, horrified.

II.

Ashore, I lead a group over the tundra, where we exclaim about the extravagance of wildflowers: monkshood most purple, roseroot crowning red, yellow saxifrage. I point out mosses and the gray, prickly lichens — how few they are, still, among the grasses and flowering plants.

Earlier, I'd briefed them about the reindeer. During World War II, when a Coast Guard station was established on the island, twenty-nine reindeer were brought over from the mainland. The station was abandoned after a year or two, but the reindeer reproduced in Malthusian fashion and by 1963 numbered some *six thousand*. They ate everything in sight and then, that brutal winter, all but forty-two starved to death. The sole surviving male was shot by a biologist committed to returning the island to its former ecology, and the final females gradually died out.

As we climb higher, the vegetation tightens toward the ground, more wind-whipped and farther from summer. Here among the berry leaves I find what I'm looking for. It's just a pale point poking free, but when I take hold of it and tug, it rips loose from the mosses. I have in hand a reindeer antler, two single prongs attached at their bases to a small white skull.

"Look at this!" I call out to my group, now spread over the hillside, on their knees with macro lenses or posing for one another against a background of anchored ship and sea. "Look at this! One of those six thousand reindeer that starved in the big die-off, forty years ago!"

Two of our group wander over to where I'm holding my find as the lovely natural object it is: elegant curves and porcelain bone, draped in moss, nibbled by voles. I am still holding it when they march on without venturing a touch, without raising their cameras. They are unimpressed with the dead thing, some poor dead animal that would only make them sad.

III.

Back on our ship, we round Glory of Russia Cape. The island on this north end rises vertically to a long, gorgeously castellated, fairy-tale ridge. In the foreground, right up against the cliffs, rests the wreck of an old freighter, broken in two and reduced to rust. The freighter was Greek, I know, the wreck only a decade ago. Imagine losing power in these faraway waters. Imagine drifting through a storm, tossed like a tin cup by enormous waves. Imagine smashing up against this rugged shore. The wreck is a monument to the indifferent ferocity of this place and to the frailty of humans and their machines.

I don't say any of this. Instead, I listen to passengers *tsk* at the rotting steel as though it's unsightly litter, a ruinous spoiling of their picture-perfect view.

A BORDER RUNS THROUGH IT

THE COMPARISONS STARTED IMMEDIATELY and
traveled the course. The mountains were huge and dramatic, with ridges and spires; they were like the northern
Rockies, as gorgeous as anything in Canada's Banff National
Park. The country was immense and full of wildlife; it was
the Tetons times ten. Domes of polished granite were shot
with waterfalls, so like Yosemite, and the meadows drifted
over with wildflowers. Glaciers hung in high valleys, above
more scoured walls; we could be in Glacier Bay. Over all,
the big western sky. And through it, winding its way down
out of a vast wilderness, came the river.

Or rivers. First, the Inklin, where it began at the juncture
of the Nahlin and Sheslay rivers. The Inklin joined with
the Yeth and with the Nakina and then became the Taku,
which met the Tulsequah and finally emptied, still among
stunning glacier-filled mountains, into Taku Inlet and then

the great Pacific, only fifteen miles from Alaska's capital city, Juneau.

Oh, yes. Somewhere in there, after the Taku and the Tulsequah joined and before the wider waters opened toward the inlet, the Taku River left one country and entered another. The river, filled with ground-up mountains and with fish, flowed out of northern British Columbia, Canada, and into southeastern Alaska, U.S.A.

We were eight — friends, friends of friends, acquaintances. We were three river boatmen, professional river rafters who had made hundreds of trips through the Grand Canyon and down dozens of North America's most challenging and scenic rivers. We were three Juneau residents, lovers of rivers and wild places. We were two more Alaskans, in shorts and Tevas, ready to work our hands to calluses in eight flowing days. We had come together to float the Taku River because none of us had.

We had come because the whole Taku River watershed — four and a half million acres of unroaded wilderness, equal to all of Massachusetts or two Yellowstone Parks — was a land that belonged to bears and their wild kin, and there were no guidebooks to tell us how to do it. The Tatshenshini, the Stikine, other Southeast Alaska rivers — those were visited and well-loved rivers. The Taku was not.

We had come, also, because of the mine.

On the Tulsequah River, the tributary that met the Taku just half a dozen miles across the U.S.-Canada border, a multi-metal underground mine was in 2004 in the final stages of review by the Canadian government. Plans by the British Columbia–based Redfern Resources Ltd. — already approved by the provincial government — called for producing 2,466 tons of ore per day for at least nine years and to employ two hundred people at the mine, the Tulsequah Chief. The sought-after deposits included zinc, copper, lead, silver, and gold. Plans for the mine also involved building a hundred-mile access road, with seventy stream crossings, to connect to the town of Atlin, British Columbia.

❧

Our first days on the river, we dwelled slowly in the country — the deep interior we'd flown through cloud-shrouded mountains to reach and so different from the coast we would soon enough return to. Despite the rain that greeted our arrival, the land was dry and crackly, a boreal landscape of spruce and aspen and the cottony seed heads of dryas flowers. On a ridge overlooking the river we pinched the leaves from sage bushes and breathed their desert smell. Flocks of waxwings swept through the trees, and eagles soared overhead. The air was soft with July heat, and the vistas were soft, too — hazy with smoke from forest fires farther inland. We were in wilderness, well beyond the reach of roads or the casual occupation by humans, and we knew that the river only ran one way — away, downstream, back. The miles were short enough — just over one hundred from our put-in place by a scrubby air-strip belonging to a remote and uninhabited homestead to our takeout just short of the ocean — and the river was high and fast. We needed to pace ourselves.

On day one, we floated all of a quarter mile, to find a perfect river-side bench padded with mattress-soft vegetation and all the firewood we could wish for. We ate our first salmon from the river and watched the sun perch like an orange ball on a mountaintop before clouds the color of our blackened cook pots rolled downriver with thunderclaps and winds that set our tents flapping.

The next day, before pushing off in our three rafts, we hiked along the river and into the woods, past aspen marked with the claws of climbing bears. We took to the river for a mile, stopped to clamber up a hillside, rounded another river bend, stopped at a clear tributary where the mud was patterned with fresh tracks — wolf, bear, moose. People used the place, too. Just up the creek we discovered a hunting camp with newly built tent platforms and a pair of shiny aluminum skiffs. Elsewhere, in the center of a bush, we found an old, rusted, leg-hold trap. We climbed higher to sit among soapberries and on rocky ledges to watch the silty, gray river twist and turn below us. We caught Dolly Varden, and then we camped and ate them, crisp-skinned and smoky-flavored.

Hot weather had recently flooded the Inklin's tributaries with snow-melt, washing freshly torn-up plants and trees onto muddy banks and into logjams. At first nervous about the current and the possibility of crashing into sweepers, I was soon taking my turn with the long oars, learning from our boatmen how to point the raft crosswise to the current, how to stay in the current as the river bent one way and another, how to look ahead and "read" the river for its rocks and eddies. I pushed and I pulled, muscling the loaded boat into position so that the river could do the main work of moving it forward. I learned that keeping dry was not an objective; we slapped through rapids and took plenty of water over the bow, we bailed, and we — in our synthetic, oil-based clothes — dried out. The sun beat down and burned the tops of my feet.

There were eagles everywhere. Their nests weighted the branches of tall cottonwood trees.

There was a fish in a tree. I didn't see it, I admit, but those who did swore to it — a large fish, a big salmon, draped over a high branch. An eagle must have set it there.

The river silt, the glacial flour finely ground, rubbed on our boat bottoms with a sound like sizzling bacon.

We floated through a charred landscape, the trees before us burned black, toppled like matchsticks over the regreening hills. We floated out of the old burn and alongside lush spruce forest, birches replacing aspen, vine maples with reddening leaves, dense devil's club, raspberries thick on their canes. We surprised browsing brown bears that were gone with the splash of an oar. The river widened, and the mountains still towered over us.

We worked at finding ideal campsites. Dry enough. Soft enough. Large enough for tent privacy. Good kitchen areas, away from tents, and with ample firewood and seating. Good views. Everything away from bear trails and heavy bear use. Clear water, if possible, or we would need to stock up on drinking water first, at one of the side creeks. Sandy places for swimming and washing. Eddies for fishing. Roots to dig for the baskets John wove as we sat around campfires into the nights.

We found them, those perfect camping places, each one different, each with its unique surprises and ample pleasures. We camped and ate in style, as one can when a boat is your workhorse, loaded with more food than you will ever need, a kitchen table, a propane stove, a tablecloth, a Dutch oven for baking cakes, ice for margaritas. Dwarf fireweed burst from the sand in purple bunches. A black bear angled down the hillside across the river from us, a long time in view, an evening's worth of entertainment. We spotted mountain goats on the sides of cliffs and beavers in sloughs, and we collected pieces of driftwood that looked like animal heads. John mixed plaster and poured it into bear tracks, later popped out molds with treacherously long claws.

With each camp departure, we dumped our fire's ash from its metal sheet into the river and swept the area clean. We left nothing but footprints and flattened grasses, the occasional relocated rock. Once we left the results of our rock contest — eight favorite rocks lined up on a log, little piles of twigs beside each to represent the allocation of our votes for best in show.

On the fourth day, the river narrowed and steepened to pour through a slot canyon — our fastest water yet and a true rollercoaster of a ride. The canyon walls were like something out of the desert Southwest — red as baked clay, with their ancient seabed layers folded and refolded into tortured swirls. We managed to "eddy out" at the seductive mouth of a side canyon, cool and mossy and overhung with drippy granite slabs, and waded up its burbling creek.

We stopped at the Yeth River, a place known for its gatherings of brown bears, who came to feed on salmon. Their tracks were everywhere around us as we debated the pros and cons of camping among bears. The argument that won out had to do neither with our safety nor our desire to see bears — of which, so far, we had seen only retreating hind ends. We decided, instead, that the bears would be best served by our absence. We caught a dinner sockeye and moved on to a sandy midstream island.

જ

Where the Inklin met the Nakina River, we reached the Taku River proper, formed by the merger of the two. Halfway through our miles, we pulled ashore to look at two Tlingit burial houses, marked with wooden crosses and weathered to a slate gray, that leaned through the alders on one bank of the Nakina. We were reminded of the Native people who have called the Taku region home for centuries and relied on the river for their transportation and trade routes, as well as for food. Canada's Taku River Tlingit once summered here in force at a major fish camp and still make regular visits; indeed, the Taku River Tlingit First Nation claims much of the Taku watershed as its traditional territory.

Slowly we were transitioning from the inland country to a more familiar coastal environment, with widening valleys and mountains hung with remnant glaciers — an even grander landscape than the grand ones we'd left behind. The glacially polished rock walls, so like those in Tracy Arm and Glacier Bay, led to the high, sharp peaks — the refugia that had never been covered, and rounded, by ice. We picked our way through braiding channels and past logjams. A harbor seal popped up in front of us, testifying to our ocean connection and the draw of salmon. When we camped on yet another idyllic island, the evening slant of sun through still-smoky skies bathed everything in soft, golden light. Arctic terns hovered and dived and shrilled to one another.

When we thought it couldn't get any better, it did. We floated through and past broad valleys until the river carried us to the one area where it rubbed up against mountain, a place marked on our map as Yellow Bluff. There we tied our boats at the base and scrambled up a goat trail, across sloping granite ledges, higher and higher to a lookout edge. The river beneath us curled into a smooth, gray ribbon, and the country was huge all around. Across the river a tremendous waterfall — Bishop Falls, 1,600 feet high — thundered down the mountainside.

We grilled salmon again, abandoning the canned chicken and other store-bought dinners to the bottom of our food boxes. Salmon are everything to the Taku, one of the top five salmon producers in Alaska. Taku salmon sustain the bears and the eagles and the trout, and the rest of what prospers in the river and along its course. They sustain the hundreds of commercial fishermen who fish for them with net and line, and the communities where those fishermen live. They sustain Juneau, whose businesses take in millions of dollars annually from sport fishing tied directly to the Taku salmon. And the Taku salmon have always sustained the Tlingit people; it's salmon, and their value in food and trade, that allowed the traditional Tlingit to live so far above the survival level, in a richly textured culture involving elaborate art, oratory, and ceremonial life.

Around the campfire, our talk was laden with superlatives. In Alaska, we're used to grand, but we all agreed that what we were seeing was grandest. The country was magnificent. Incredibly spectacular. Mindblowing. Jaw-dropping. Majorly impressive in its wildlife. Rich. Huge. Vast. Awe-inspiring. Amazingly wild.

The fact that the Taku was just *there* — in Juneau's backyard — and that it was without any special designation or protective status was as mind-blowing as the scenery.

Thad, our quiet boatman, spoke up. "It's like Glen Canyon, the place that no one knew," he said, referencing the Colorado River canyon that was lost beneath Lake Powell when the Glen Canyon Dam was built half a century ago. "Now conservationists regret that they let that go."

༄

And then we met the Tulsequah River, flowing in on our right. We stopped for a leg-stretcher along its freshly flooded shoreline and to get a better look at the distant Tulsequah Glacier pouring out of a high valley. Only later would we learn that the glacially dammed Tulsequah Lake had three weeks earlier experienced an outburst flood, an event that occurs when summer rains and meltwater break through the ice dam. The U. S. Geological Survey has warned that the annual Tulsequah outburst "is a potentially dangerous and destructive flood that may affect inhabitants of the Taku and Tulsequah River Valleys. As this area becomes developed, the frequency and magnitude of outburst floods are of great concern."

The Tulsequah Chief mine, just downstream of the glacier and lake, lay another ten miles beyond where we stopped to study mountain goats with our binoculars. The old mine at the site, to be reopened and enlarged, hasn't operated since 1957 but continues to leak acid pollution and heavy metals. Had we hiked all the way to the mine site, we would have seen the old mine's brown scars and orange stain blooming out into the river water. We would also have seen renewed activity in the area — a new Redfern camp, workers and equipment, signs of exploratory drilling from the last two field seasons. With provincial approval in hand, Redfern only needed federal certification from Ottawa to begin its development. Even as we walked beside the river, the Canadian government was in the midst of a formal — and fast-tracked — review.

Despite downstream issues regarding water quality, fisheries, and people, and despite available mechanisms for addressing transboundary issues, the United States and Alaska had had little say about the proposed mine. The U. S. Environmental Protection Agency, State Department, and Department of the Interior all had registered concerns in past years and attempted to negotiate a watershed planning effort. Then, under the Bush administration, the Department of the Interior removed its objections and essentially halted the efforts toward a binational resolution. In a similar political shift, Alaska's efforts to get a review of the project by the International Joint Commission, an independent body established under the authority of the Boundary Waters Treaty of 1909 to resolve disputes between the United States and Canada on boundary water issues and meant to protect both countries from contamination by each other, ended when Governor Frank Murkowski, a Republican, was elected in 2002. Governor Murkowski, who advocated road development in the Taku area, weakened Alaska's water quality standards to allow the pollution of salmon streams.

Meanwhile, local legislators, environmentalists, fishermen, Tlingit tribal people from both sides of the border, and a number of Taku River cabin owners offered up long lists of concerns they said had not been addressed. In their nightmare version of the future, mine operations and their wastes would degrade water quality and take down a multimillion-dollar salmon industry, the road would invite more mining and other development in a de facto wilderness and increase hunting and fishing pressures, and the total package of access and development would overrun the traditional homelands (and their subsistence and cultural values) of the Tlingit people. They pointed out that another half-dozen mines currently being explored in the area awaited a determination on Tulsequah Chief and access issues before moving forward; road access would be key to their economic viability.

Chris Zimmer, U.S. coordinator for the Transboundary Watershed Alliance (now Rivers Without Borders), which represented twenty-two conservation organizations on both sides of the border, continued to press for a more public and binational process and was particularly incensed by the failure of Redfern to clean up the existing mine pollution. "The long history of ignoring Alaska's interests in the Taku clearly demonstrates why we can't trust B.C. and Redfern to protect water quality and fisheries," he has argued. He also complained to me that Alaska was getting more like British Columbia — that is, willing to weaken environmental standards and cut back on regulation and enforcement, in the pursuit of economic development.

Kat Hall, water quality and mining organizer for the Southeast Alaska Conservation Council, based in Juneau, was even more direct with me. "A salmon fishery worth over ten million dollars annually to local commercial and sport fishermen is being put at risk for a mine in which *all* the benefits would go across the border. Clearly, B.C. gets the mine and Alaska gets the shaft."

The permitting process would take longer than any of us expected, as questionable economics stalled the project and burgeoning metal prices restarted it. The feared road access was eventually replaced with a plan to use air-cushioned barges on the Taku River, arousing even more concern from Taku River fishermen and others who depend on the river. And still the studies and permitting continued.

※

The Taku is famous for winds that blow upriver, and we battled gusts that slowed us to a crawl as the river ever widened. Occasional cabins, with skiffs parked before them like cars at curbs, appeared to our left and our right, and salmon gillnets hung drying on racks. Debris — including entire leafy cottonwood trees — was piled in jams at the river's bends.

I had not expected an actual line between Canada and the United States, but there it was: a cleared fifty-foot swath straight down a mountainside, and, just in case you missed the meaning, a cement barrel, marked with the countries' names, on the shore at river's edge.

In a narrow passage on the Alaska side, two fish wheels — counting salmon — turned with the current. We pulled and paddled past cabins and more cabins, a noisy congestion of people careening by us in skiffs or chainsawing firewood in their yards; it was a Saturday, recreation time for Juneau residents who — many of them — have held Taku River cabin sites in their families for generations. Who would not love that river at the door, the mountains and their blue glaciers looking down?

We were tempted by Twin Glaciers, approachable from the river, but our progress against the wind was too painfully slow. We satisfied ourselves with a clear view of the outstretched Devils Paw Mountain and pulled on toward the front of Hole-in-the-Wall, a branch of the giant Taku Glacier. The historic Taku Lodge, across the now broad and very shallow, estuarine river, beckoned.

Float planes delivering camera-toting tourists for a salmon bake at the lodge hauled us home. In fifteen minutes we flew past glaciers and ice field, over the tide-filling Taku Inlet, across a mountain pass to Gastineau Channel just south of Juneau. We coasted in beside an enormous cruise ship and locked eyes with upper-deck passengers lounging on balconies. It's right there, I wanted to tell them. There's a magical place, so close to us, so physically near. And so close to becoming, before you know the first thing about it, something entirely else.

THE CONSERVATIONIST
AS WOOD CHOPPER

THIS USED TO BE SELF-EVIDENT: whales needed to be saved. Whaling was, by definition, something to be stopped. When I was growing up in the 1960s, whaling fleets composed of catcher boats and factory ships still operated throughout the oceans in an essentially unregulated way, and many species of large whales were in danger of going extinct. Who would *not* want to save the whales— and the eagles, wolves, redwood trees, polluted rivers, and all the rest of our precious and abused natural heritage that the whales, such magnificent creatures, represented? The earth was being treated very badly, and the whales symbolized all that was wrong and all that might be restored.

After we moved to Alaska in 1973 Ken and I for several years operated an outdoors store that sold camping gear and clothing. We gladly joined in the boycott of Norwegian- and Japanese-made products to express our displeasure with the killing of whales. I remember myself huddled over supply catalogs, checking the origin of zippers in sleeping bags and jackets. I was so pleased with myself for helping whales and the environment.

Today—older, more experienced with both natural and political systems, perhaps wiser, or at least more realistic than my young self— I've learned that few things in life are as simple as we'd like them to be. *If only* we could save the world by saving the whales. I'm not so sure anymore about the single-minded focus of the anti-whaling campaign, and I question how well it's serving even whales. But let me explain.

༄

You can love what you kill and eat. I've spent much of my adult life catching salmon destined for someone's dinner plate. I love salmon, and yet I kill them, because I know that the stocks from which they come are well-managed and sustainable, and that salmon are a healthful food. When I say I love salmon, I don't mean that I love to eat them (although I do), but that I love them for what they are and their role in the universe. When I look at a salmon leaping from the ocean I see an animal of great and shining beauty, and when I look at a salmon in the bottom of my boat I admire the lines of it and the colors that match the waters of its home river. I know that other commercial fishermen feel a similar attraction and, through this intimate relationship, know the natural world—its cycles and harsh realities—in a way that has largely been lost from modern life. Fishermen know the fish's death as the final flop and blood spilling from a gill, or as the tattered, fungus-covered spawner floating past. Death is never pretty.

Farmers, ranchers, and others who live close to the land share a similar familiarity with the natural world, as do, of course, people who maintain traditional lives involving hunting and gathering. My worldview has certainly been shaped by association with Alaska Natives who, even as they modernize, own in their core values beliefs that animals present themselves as gifts to the hunters who show them respect, and that a lack of respect will cause the animals to withhold themselves.

Along with salmon, I love the small white whales, belugas, that chase and feed upon salmon. I love beluga whales so much that when I saw the population in my region (Alaska's Cook Inlet) disappearing, I wrote a book about them and their place in the ecosystem, including its human elements, that surrounds them. I didn't hesitate to condemn the overhunting (by Alaska Natives) and the mismanagement (by the National Marine Fisheries Service) that resulted in their depletion, and I continue to advocate for their protection.

I also visited an Inupiat village in Alaska's Arctic, where a yearly hunt of beluga whales (from a large and stable population) provides the people with much of their food. I was impressed with the self-management by the hunters (who decided how to conduct the hunt and how many whales to take, within guidelines worked out by a larger hunter and biologist group to which they belonged) and witnessed the significance of the hunt in reinforcing community values as well as providing traditional food.

Later, a review of my book in the Animal Welfare Institute's *AWI Quarterly* asked "How can the author love these whales and care passionately about their protection yet feel so little empathy when they are hurt and killed in front of her?" And, "It was as if the author loved churches but never 'got' religion."

To which I would like to finally respond: my religion differs from that of the reviewer. He would hold me to a single religion—his—in the same way that some fundamentalists allow no room for beliefs other than their own. I belong to the church of sky and sea and am a disciple of (among others) Aldo Leopold, who said the best definition of a conservationist was written not with a pen but with an axe—"a matter of what a man thinks about while chopping, or while deciding what to chop."

※

Distinctions are important. Whales are not big fish, although in the Moby-Dick days people thought of them that way, as just another creature to be caught in a "fishery." Whales are also not human, although some of our kind think of them as beings that rival, or perhaps exceed, humans in intelligence. It is true that whales have large brains, most likely needed for navigation and communication, but, scientists warn, not necessarily linked to intelligence as we know it. Whales participate in complex social arrangements, but so do ants and bees. Discoveries that birds use tools and octopuses can learn to unscrew lids from jars suggest that many animals—not just large mammals—have specialized skills formerly attributed to only the "highly evolved."

Whales are not all the same, and not all are endangered. Some whale species—blue, humpback, bowhead, right—*are* endangered and clearly need continued protections. Other species—or populations within them—have rebounded to numbers that may match or even exceed those that existed historically, before the commercial whaling era. (Pre-exploitation numbers have been difficult to establish, and I'm fascinated with the developing field of genetic markers, which can trace lineages and suggest the breadth of ancestor pools based on time and divergence.)

All whaling is not the same. Under the management regime of the International Whaling Commission (IWC), "aboriginal" whaling is allowed by certain groups for food. In Alaska and Russia, this means that Native hunters may take, in the next five-year period, up to 280 bowhead whales (an endangered species but from a population showing steady growth) and up to 620 gray whales for their subsistence purposes. Smaller numbers of whales, including minke, fin, and humpback, are allocated to a few other traditional whale-hunting peoples.

Commercial whaling, involving the exchange of whale products and money, is prohibited by the IWC under a moratorium adopted in 1982.

Japan and its allies argue that another kind of whaling—which they call small-type, coastal, or community-based—should be allowed and is similar to subsistence whaling in that it would be conducted by communities with long whaling traditions to feed local people. The difference is that, in this case, the whalers don't qualify as aboriginal and their past activity involved selling whale meat for profit.

Meanwhile, limited (and legal) commercial whaling is conducted by countries (Norway and Iceland) that filed reservations to the moratorium, an opt-out option allowed under IWC rules. Canada, which left the IWC in 1982 to protest the moratorium, manages whaling by its Inuit people apart from IWC oversight. The whaling of small cetaceans (like belugas) occurs outside of the IWC altogether, per each country's own rules.

One category of whaling deserves a separate emphasis. Officially known as special-permit whaling, it's generally referred to as "scientific" whaling, placed in quotation marks to indicate its controversy. Per the original whaling convention, any country may kill whales as part of its scientific research. Japan's research program—which took 859 whales, mostly minkes, in 2006—is generally considered a sham. Although a certain amount of useful information about stock compositions, diets, and animal health is obtained, the program seems to be an act of defiance and potential bargaining strategy on Japan's part. The whale meat ends up in markets and school lunches.

Finally, I wish to note the deep philosophical differences between conservation and preservation, and between conservation and support of animal rights. Conservation does not preclude the use of living resources (including whales) on a sustainable basis. Preservation is based on a no-take policy, whether old-growth forest or whales are involved. The animal rights movement adheres to an ethical belief that whale killing is simply wrong. While conservation based on scientific analysis and sustainable use principles is embraced by international law, nations (and people within nations) hold varying attitudes toward the consumptive use of animals.

❧

There's history and geopolitics to all this. The current state of whales, whaling, and anti-whaling cannot be understood without knowing how we came to this conflicted place.

The use of whales for food and other purposes—for example, rib bones used in place of wooden timbers in the homes of northern peoples—goes back thousands of years. From coastal and shore whaling, the effort expanded to long sea journeys by sailing and, eventually, steam-driven ships. The infamous high-seas commercial whaling focused principally on whale oil used for lighting, with the industry's excess beginning in the early 1800s and targeting different species in succession as one after another was "fished out." New whaling technologies—and the need to pay for the capitalization of expensive fleets—kept the industry going at a level beyond either need or justification. The fact that whales traveled the oceans and belonged to no single nations meant that their conservation required international cooperation.

And so it was that the United States led the way, post–World War II, to negotiate the International Convention for the Regulation of Whaling "to provide for the proper conservation of whale stocks and thus make possible the orderly development of the whaling industry." With its initial fourteen whaling-nation members, the International Whaling Commission for many years did a very poor job of regulation and allowed whaling to continue at unsustainable levels. In the mid-1970s, the organization finally banned the whaling of all overexploited whales while allowing catches of abundant stocks at levels that wouldn't threaten their existence. But by that time anti-whaling forces were gathering the votes to adopt the moratorium on all commercial whaling, which went into effect in 1986.

Thus we sit, with nations that opted out of the moratorium or left the IWC altogether continuing modest levels of whaling, others making use of the "scientific" loophole, Japan bringing its same requests for coastal whaling to the IWC year after year in what has become a ritual, and the organization's scientific committee continuing to evaluate the strengths of various whale stocks and work up management plans that are never implemented. The IWC now has seventy-six member nations, most of them without any whaling history (some without even any coastline) but recruited to the organization by one side or the other. Dominated by its anti-whaling membership, the IWC neither addresses its mandate ("the orderly development of the whaling industry") nor has reinvented itself to any agreed-upon purpose. It is generally considered to be dysfunctional, irrelevant, and divisive.

I attest to this conclusion firsthand, after attending the 2007 IWC annual meeting, which met in Anchorage. While the four-day meeting began with a lot of rhetoric about building trust and working cooperatively, the situation quickly deteriorated. Commissioners were soon accusing one another of bad faith, disrespect, grandstanding, and misrepresenting or ignoring the science involved. In the end, many reports were presented, aboriginal quotas were continued, a few resolutions were adopted, and a specific agenda item called "The Future of the IWC" resulted in some thoughtful discussion, but the polarization continued. Japan got nowhere with its bid for "normalization" (code for a return to the organization's whaling mission) and its request for four coastal villages to take a limited number of minke whales for food. The anti-whaling faction talked about "modernization" of the IWC but lacked the three-quarters vote needed to create a whale sanctuary in the South Atlantic. Within a resolution approved by a slim majority, the commission reaffirmed the moratorium—stating that the reasons for it were still valid. (This was a reversal of another slimly passed declaration from the previous meeting, which suggested that the moratorium might one day end and be replaced by a system of limited and controlled whaling.)

As with any political entity, much of what goes on at the IWC is offstage, in private discussions and negotiations, and the surfaces are not always what they look to be. In particular I felt at a loss to judge whether the commissioner from Japan was making genuine appeals to the others or, perhaps, playing more to his domestic audience. His presentation and requests to the body were only slightly different from those Japan has been making for years and which have, for years, always been rejected. I had to wonder whether his demonstrative disappointment in the end was based on reasonable expectations of what might have been possible or had more to do with expressing his nation's sense of pride and victimization.

What became most clear to me was the deep divide within the organization and the alignment of interests. On one side stood the anti-whaling countries, which also generally correspond to the world's economic and political giants. On the other side stood the nations with whaling traditions they wish to continue joined by numbers of less powerful nations that voiced what seemed to me legitimate concerns about food security, national autonomy, and the rules of the game. I had the uncomfortable feeling that nations that see themselves as "more advanced" thought that other nations were simply backward and would come to share their enlightened positions about the value of whales if they would only sharpen up their thinking.

One moment disturbs me above all others. During a presentation by Denmark to support a request to add a few whales to Greenland's aboriginal quota, the man sitting next to me kept snickering. The presenter was making what, to me, was a reasonable case: increasing whale stocks, the environmental advantage of using local resources instead of importing foods, the health benefits of traditional foods. The man next to me, whose briefcase bore the sticker of an animal rights group, muttered under his breath, "So buy tractors."

ン

Times change.

Attitudes about whales and whaling and about other animals and the proper relationships humans should have with them have, like almost everything else, changed with time.

Most people today don't need or desire to eat whale meat. They don't need whale oil for their lights or lubrication, nor baleen for corset stays. They do—judging from the explosive growth of the whale-watching business—enjoy seeing whales in the wild. It has become commonplace to say, "A live whale is worth more than a dead whale," recognizing the economic value of the whale-watching industry. Indeed, I've seen plenty of Alaska's tourists shout with joy when humpback and fin whales surface beside them. I may not be a shouter, but I feel the same thrill—I mean, who's *not* impressed by a large, sleek, beautiful, and mysterious whale?

Competing polls show that Americans are opposed to commercial whaling or, when asked more nuanced questions about the regulated take of non-endangered species like minkes, are in favor of limited and sustainable whaling. (I have to wonder: how many Americans would recognize a minke whale, or could tell you the first thing about its biology, distribution, or numbers?)

Even in whaling countries, the appetite for whale products may be diminishing. The Japanese themselves have turned away from whale meat (as they have turned away from a fish and rice diet), despite their government's efforts to promote it as a part of the country's heritage and food culture. Much of the meat from their "scientific" catches is now served in school lunches with ketchup. Iceland recently found that there was little market for the few whales taken by its whalers, and the fisheries minister stopped the hunting until more demand could justify it. Around the world, the people and communities who had been involved in whaling before the moratorium, now a generation out, have largely moved on to new employment and economies, if not identities.

Even in subsistence whale-hunting cultures like Alaska's, the traditions grow weaker. While the cultural importance of the hunt and sharing in and among communities is without debate, the hunters and their families increasingly participate in a cash economy and enjoy a varied diet. After the burst of feasting to celebrate a whale hunt, young people especially return to something closer to an all-American diet of pizza and Pop-Tarts.

It's possible that, with time, our globalized culture will turn entirely away from consumptive use of whales. Then the IWC will be truly irrelevant.

But it's one thing to watch globalization diminish the vitality of individual cultures, and another thing to impose the values of dominant cultures on others—which can only be described as cultural imperialism and lead to the kind of resentment I witnessed at the IWC meeting. Consider again the case that the whaling countries make: let all abide by scientific principles regarding conservation and sustained use of resources, and let each nation made autonomous management decisions within international law. Is that not just?

As the commissioner from Russia put it, the problem the whaling countries have in providing traditional foods to their people is caught "in the meat grinder of politics." The commissioner from the Caribbean nation of St. Lucia put it even more starkly: "We need to understand one another. The alternative leads to war."

Times change, yes. The old system of rapacious commercial whaling is rightly rejected—but also, given today's economics, regulatory mechanisms, and public awareness—beyond any reasonable risk of being returned to. The ogre of "commercial whaling" today serves only as a straw argument.

Might not an acceptance of regulated, sustainable whaling crack open, not a return to the past, but future potentials? Consider: bringing back to the management fold the alienated and opted-out whaling nations, ending the charade of "scientific" whaling, quitting the hypocrisy of allowing some coastal people to hunt endangered whales while prohibiting other coastal people from hunting plentiful whales. And could not the many nongovernmental organizations that have devoted themselves for so long to the cause of whales apply their energies to greater purpose?

⚘

Forgive the expression, but at this point all of us have bigger fish to fry.

As important as whales are, and as important as the IWC is or should be as an international conservation organization, the crises of our modern world make debates over the hunting of individual whales an indulgence.

Much larger issues confront whales and our oceans. If the IWC spent less time wrangling, it could bring focus to research and management needs and to addressing pollution, habitat loss, fishing conflicts, and, most urgently, global warming and its evil twin, ocean acidification. Degraded oceans will not support the whale populations we would all like to see thrive.

And if our own species is going to survive on this earth, we need international cooperation, not just in resource conservation but in every aspect of our shared existence. Such cooperation is not going to come by the exertion of political dominance but by respecting the sovereignty of other nations and their rights to hold independent views.

In a 1999 *Atlantic Monthly* opinion piece, William Aron, a former U.S. commissioner to the IWC, and two of his scientific colleagues wrote that banning whaling on moral rather than scientific grounds has caused a "bitter stand-off [that] violates international law, fosters tensions between otherwise friendly nations, and undermines environmental legislation." Worst of all, they wrote, was the danger that nations would shy away from future multilateral agreements for fear the U.S. and its allies would later "move the goalposts" with new interpretations of agreed-upon principles or even sanctions against actions allowed by law or treaty.

A decade later, we endure the same stalemated IWC and its culture of distrust. With an eleventh-hour recognition of the global warming crisis, the need for international cooperation on environmental issues should be obvious to all. If we truly want to save whales, I suggest we start by trying to save a science-based system of international regulation that—by keeping the big picture of global health foremost in our intentions—might yet become a model for addressing the very large (indeed, leviathan) challenges ahead.

THE EXPERIMENT

IT WAS THE FIRST COLD NOVEMBER DAY, with temperatures in the twenties and a bluebird sky to backdrop the snow-covered volcanoes across the inlet. At two o'clock, when I set out for a walk in the woods, the sun was already sinking toward Cook Inlet. Heavy frost from the previous night still coated the trail and crunched underfoot like broken glass. I snapped my jacket closed at my neck, pausing to admire the way the low-level sun lit up the spent fireweed stalks and their cottony strands. *When the fireweed goes to cotton, summer's soon forgotten*. Fireweed has always acted as the Alaska calendar, the old saying hastening us through summer as the purple blossoms climb their stalks, close into seed sheathes, and — finally — pop open in a white, wind-driven flurry.

The trail I set off on I knew well, although I knew it not as a hiking trail on bare ground but as the start to many miles of winter ski loops. In recent years I've visited the trail system less often than in the past; our snow season has been beginning later and ending earlier — and too often is ruined by midwinter rains. The local newspaper had just pointed out that thirty years ago this same week in November we were digging out from a twenty-eight-inch snowstorm. I recall those snow years fondly — the fences between hayfields disappearing under drifts, the great quiet that settled over the land, skiing until Memorial Day. It may be easy to be nostalgic for the conditions of one's youth, but in fact I now inhabit a different, more temperate climatic zone. Airport weather data supply the evidence: mean winter temperatures since 1977 have increased by six degrees Fahrenheit.

The trail system starts out on state land known as the Homer Demonstration Forest, an area set aside for forestry research and education. One fenced quarter acre shelters experimental plantings of native and non-native trees and shrubs, and another fenced "exclosure" demonstrates what happens when moose are prevented from eating the natural vegetation. (Willows grow big and bushy.) Volunteers maintain the trails and a few wooden boardwalks and bridges.

I stopped in the middle of said forest to watch a pair of eagles and a raven soar in circles above me. If I had been in a true forest, of course, I wouldn't have been able to see the birds past the trees, but the demonstration forest has a problem with its forest. There are trees, yes — spruce trees — but they are bare and broken and fallen, and the sky is large in the holes around them. Forest — with its shade, undergrowth, and damp floor — has given way to sunlight, chest-high grasses, and fireweed. The forest is turning to grassland.

A newly fallen spruce lay broken beside the path, its splintered wood a warm yellow, dry and punky. The tree had not been dead long, and its bark still clung tightly, sticky with globs and drips of pitch.

This has become typical forest for Alaska's Kenai Peninsula — that is, dead spruce trees, needleless and dry, brittle, blowing down in every windstorm. The mature and even the much younger spruce of the region — white, Sitka, and the dominant hybrid known as Lutz — are almost entirely dead now, killed by a spruce bark beetle epidemic that began in the 1980s and swept through four million acres in the 1990s. This death by beetle is said to be the single largest insect kill ever recorded in North America. When I flew over the peninsula in the beetle-spreading years, I looked down on whole sections of forest tinged red — recently killed, with needles turned to rust — and then the next year I saw those sections gone gray and the red spread farther, and then, in a few years, what I witnessed were the gray trees snapped off and lying over the country like toothpicks tossed down by a giant. Then the logging roads came, cutting up the land and silting the creeks, and trees were mowed down and hauled off as wood chips to become Asian newsprint.

Hiking again, I peered under still-standing trees to where the mossy forest floor was littered with cones and twigs, with oak ferns and species of *Pyrola*, the wintergreens that hold their color through the snow season, the better to get a start on spring. Trees that had fallen across the trail had been bucked up and dragged to the sides. I remembered when the beetle plague first spread and the blame was assigned to poor logging practices. The forestry experts declared that when trees were cleared for home sites and power lines, the downed trees became havens for the rice-grain-sized beetles, which reproduced in them and then struck living trees. The solution, those experts said, was to buck the cleared trees into short lengths, because then the wood would dry out and discourage the beetles.

It took years for anyone to understand the severity of the beetle attack, and longer to grasp the cause. Spruce bark beetles are a natural part of our environment, and the records of tree rings and lake pollen show that they have regularly — every fifty years or so — thinned the forest. In our wet climate they are thought to be *the* force — instead of fire — for regenerating forest lands. They play a very useful role in decomposing dead wood. However, nothing in any record suggests that they have ever before been so successful in killing off entire forests.

This is the question: what happens when you increase air temperatures by several degrees? I've used the word *you* because I mean *you*, *me*, the humans who, through our activities since the beginning of the Industrial Age, have added so much carbon dioxide and other greenhouse gasses to the atmosphere that temperatures have warmed by one degree Fahrenheit globally and considerably more toward the earth's poles. The answer in my home place is this: trees accustomed to cooler temperatures and greater moisture become stressed and thus more vulnerable to pests and disease, while bark beetles, previously held in check by cold winters and cool summers, flourish. The beetles are able to complete their life cycle in one year instead of two, and the summers that make us sweat present them with the perfect warmth for mating flights and egg laying.

At another turn in the trail, I rested my hand on another downed tree, its splintered wood faded to gray. The bark that wasn't already scabbed off was peppered with beetle holes. I pulled away a piece to expose the labyrinthine galleries left by the beetle larvae as they ate their way through the tree's phloem. When a spruce's phloem, between the bark and the wood, is no longer intact enough to move nutrients throughout the tree, the tree essentially starves.

I thought about the summers when the beetles were at their worst, and the hot days that brought them out of the trees to fly in clouds across the land. We brushed them from our clothes and tried not to inhale. We fled the outdoors and made comparisons to Alfred Hitchcock birds and Biblical plagues.

That summer horror has lessened now, only because the beetles finally ran out of food. Without the trees to support them, they faced their own death — or flew to farther forests.

To be sure, not every tree in the demonstration forest is dead. Here and there along my way middle-age spruces still spread their living needles, still sported clusters of cones. And along the trail edges and in new openings that hadn't filled with grass, hundreds of baby spruce trees, like miniature Christmas trees a foot or so high, were springing up. A few among the recruits were tagged with yellow or orange flags, part of a study that involved some plantings and some natural reseeding, in different locations, on nurse logs or in scarified areas where mineral soil was exposed.

One of these flagged areas lay adjacent to an enormous old stump, two feet across, rotten in its center and clothed with lichens. Enough surface was still visible for me to count fifteen or twenty growth rings to an average inch. Ring records don't just tell us the age of trees but show, in old trees, patterns of tight and wider rings corresponding to a history of forest conditions — moisture and drought, sun and shade. Foresters can typically track the "releases" of greater growth corresponding to periods when neighboring trees died and fell away, decreasing competition for space, light, and nutrients. The old stump could show me a history of bark beetles coming and going through the forest, but I was more impressed by the tightness of the rings generally. Northern forests grow slowly, and that one tree might have been a seedling when Captain Cook gazed upon the spruce-lined shore two and a third centuries ago.

Crows and ravens flapped between trees, and a pair of magpies — *yak-yak-yak* — followed one after another through an opening. Insect-eaters — chickadees and woodpeckers — have done well in the dying and dead forest, and the omnivorous magpies seem to be everywhere. Magpies favor disturbed areas, including open woods and fields, and they are significant predators of other birds' eggs and young. According to bird sighting records, their numbers have increased mightily throughout south-central Alaska *and* they're moving northward, deeper into Alaska's interior where they have not previously been players.

I came finally to a more open area, where a wooden boardwalk crossed wetlands and grass gave way to willows and crowberry. At the edge of Diamond Creek I listened to running water and admired the lacey configurations of newly forming ice. Diamond Creek is just one of the many waterways in the region that, due to record-setting precipitation and unusually warm temperatures, suffered not one but two "hundred-year floods" in 2002. The flooding severely altered habitat, both in the stream itself and along and beside its banks. Beaver dams washed away, and the beavers themselves disappeared, presumably drowned. The Dolly Varden that lived in Diamond Creek have also disappeared, their streambed habitat scoured clean.

Diamond Creek does not support salmon, a mainstay of Alaska's economy, but neighboring streams that do are threatened by warming waters. According to Alaska's water quality standards, 55.5 degrees Fahrenheit is the upper limit for successful salmon spawning and egg survival. On the nearby Anchor River that temperature was exceeded on eighty-eight days in 2005. Moreover, temperatures of sixty-eight degrees, the assumed limits of salmon tolerance, were exceeded on six days. Biologists and fishermen were monitoring salmon health and production nervously, well aware of the situation farther west, where Yukon River king salmon have been devastated by a fungus associated with warmer water.

What happens when you increase the earth's temperatures? Warming rivers, hotter and longer summers, warmer and shorter winters, thawing permafrost, melting glaciers, thinning sea ice, drying wetlands, shrinking lakes, more wildfires, species migrating into new ranges, species facing extinction, disrupted breeding schedules, declines in food production, lighter snowpacks, eroding coastlines, displaced people, dead forests, temperature-related diseases, food stress, rising sea levels, landscape transformations, stormier weather — here in the north we've already got all this. *And* ocean acidification, not a result of warmer temperatures but of the ocean's absorption of carbon dioxide from the atmosphere — the "twin" result of our greenhouse gas emissions and a threat to every marine organism that depends on a carbonate shell.

Do you think what happens in Alaska doesn't and won't affect you? Think again. The landscape before me is your future. "Business as usual" will cause the global mean temperature to increase by between 2.5 and 10 degrees Fahrenheit by 2100, according to the scientific consensus report prepared by the Intergovernmental Panel on Climate Change, the international collaboration of thousands of scientists and the world's leading authority on climate change. The results of such rapid temperature increases, the fastest in at least ten thousand years, will be dramatic in a world already straining to provide food, water, and shelter to 6.5 billion people.

The question we're now testing might be: once a species evolves to be capable of actually changing the world's climate, can that species manage and modify its behavior to prevent the destruction of the systems that sustain it? Or will it be the agent of a mass extinction? In such an extinction, what will be the fate of that apex species? On our singular, beautiful and ravaged earth, this is an experiment without controls.

As I circled back to the trailhead, I thought about that species — so far evolved, so able, so intelligent. I thought about the clock analogy: if a twenty-four-hour clock started at the earth's beginning 4.6 billion years ago, it was already 7:15 p.m. when the first multicell plants evolved and 9:25 p.m. when the first fish swam in the oceans. The first small African apes didn't appear until 11:58 and *Homo sapiens* until 11:59:58 — two seconds ago. Perhaps we should wonder if *we* aren't the experiment, like a small test light turned on before blinking out forever.

MY APOLOGIA

THE PLAN WAS THIS: I would visit Alaska's McNeil River State Game Sanctuary and watch people being crazy about bears. I had seen plenty of bears over the years myself; I always enjoyed seeing them, but they weren't novel to me, and I wasn't gaga about them. I was interested in the people who came from all over the world to watch and photograph bears (as though there weren't already a zillion identical photos, McNeil bears starring in every calendar and wildlife magazine). I wanted to meet people who, like Timothy Treadwell's friend, Jewel Palovak (featured in the Werner Herzog film *Grizzly Man*), would wear bear-shaped earrings. I wanted to meet people who were all about feeling spiritual connections to bears, although perhaps not as emphatically as Treadwell himself who—for those who might have escaped the news—tried so hard to live with bears and be their friend that, in 2003, just down the coast from McNeil, he was finally eaten by one. (And yes, the gallows humor has it that he succeeded in becoming a bear, or at least got inside of a bear.)

I was ho-hum about bears but intrigued by people who I believed were a little too intense about things with fur, too attached to the stuffed toys of their childhoods, too unacquainted with actual wildlife. I wanted to try to understand what kind of aesthetic or meaningful experience such people found in the presence of bears.

❧

First difficulty: It's hard for anyone to say what it is that makes bears so attractive because, when you see one, all you can think, really, is *Oh, my god, look at that!*

The day that I arrived one of the Fish and Game guides met me at the camp and walked me through the sedge flats to join the group already clustered on a rise above Mikfik Creek. (This was still June. By early July the bears—and bear viewers—would congregate at the more famous McNeil Falls, up the adjacent valley.) All around us, bears were grazing the flats like cows, swinging their heads and making ripping noises as they grabbed and tore mouthfuls of greens. We wove our way through them, stopping to yield when one and another left off grazing and strolled on down the same rutted trail we were following.

One bear (sub-adult male, guide Doug informed me) changed course to approach us, stiffening his legs in what I knew was called "cowboy walk," a kind of swagger bears use to display their toughness to one another. Doug, in front of me, turned sideways to the bear, a way of looking big but not necessarily bad. The bear had a snouty, upturned face that he seemed to still be growing into, with a crease down the middle of his forehead that made him look like he was super worried about something. His eyes were hard and set perhaps overly far apart. I'm sure his fur was really beautiful, but I was only looking at his face and the piece of tongue hanging out of his mouth.

I had been reading a book about Timothy Treadwell (*The Grizzly Maze*, by Nick Jans), perhaps not the ideal book for the occasion.

I hadn't even gotten to the part about the screams (recorded in the Treadwell tent by a capped video camera), but I knew the story and was horrified every time I thought of Timothy's poor girlfriend, Amie Huguenard, trying to fend off the killer bear with a frying pan before following Timothy into his same (some say suicidal) fate.

I waited behind Doug. The bear, puffed up like a Hitler youth, walked away.

From across the valley the colorful group of bear watchers, standing among camera tripods, looked back at us and at the bears fishing in the creek, as a sow with two trailing cubs passed just a few feet behind them.

Nearby, two bears were busy mating, appearing exactly like an obscene ivory carving I'd once seen in a gift shop, only animated, with the spasmodic male bear biting at the female's neck.

All up and down the valley the impossibly green sedges undulated in the wind like a single living organism. The creek, with a thick margin of muddy bank, reflected a pastel sky. White heads of eagles glowed from the top of the opposite cliffs, and the rolling, treeless country beyond reached into mountains still streaked with snow. And everywhere—*Ursus arctos*, the coastal brown bear. The sounds of them splashing after salmon and of their huffing and growling floated across the flats.

"This is amazing," I said, feebly.

❧

Basic fact: McNeil is not about scare-bears. It's not about interacting with bears at all, which is why that little bit of cowboy drama my first day was unusual. Since the sanctuary was created in 1967, the idea has been to avoid interfering with what is known as the world's largest concentration of wild brown bears. For more than thirty years now, human access has been strictly limited; these days a maximum of ten visitors at a time, chosen by lottery for four-day periods, are accompanied by bear-savvy Fish and Game employees to regular viewing spots for watching the bears that gather to feed on salmon.

The phrase the biologists use is "neutral habituation." The bears learn that people will be clumped together in certain spots or walking in a line between points, but they associate those people neither with danger (which might make them nervous or even cause them to run away) nor with food (which might make them approach, hoping for a sandwich and cookies).

Over the generations of bears, the guides have come to know individual bears and their particular behaviors—who's dominant, who hangs out with whom, who catches fish by the lunge method as opposed to the snorkel method as opposed to stealing fish from other bears. They know how much personal space a particular bear needs.

In theory, the bears ignore the people who watch them. With so much of their favorite foods available, and with the imperative to eat heartily and put on as much weight as possible, they're all about being eating machines. (Despite the Treadwell example just given, bears generally have no interest in eating people; the rare attack is almost always defensive.) In practice, the bears have found people to be occasionally interesting, and occasionally useful.

Another day, walking up the valley in a small group, we stopped short of a grazing sow and her cub—not a "cub of the year" born that winter in the den but a year beyond that, an age that still keeps close to mama's heels. The sow kept grazing toward us, and the cub kept up a steady whining that anyone—even a human—could decipher as *Waa! Waa! Waa! I'm hungry! Right now!* Mother bear was not hearing that. She grazed closer and closer to us as the cub head-butted her and cried so pitifully. Then, noticing us, the cub—its little face full of curiosity and perhaps expectation—made a beeline for us.

This is where you remember all the stories about the dangers of getting between a mother bear and her cub.

That cub came within a hand's reach while guide Ian spoke softly to it (some discouraging words), crouched low, and finally waved his cap in its face, which made it back up. It butted its mother again and cried, bit at some sedges like a kid proving that he *had* tried his broccoli, came back to us. We repeated this sequence a few more times, with Mama barely looking up. Finally Mama led Cubby up the bluff; when we passed under a short time later, we could see her sprawled out on her back, with the furiously nursing cub pummeling her chest.

Writer to self: *Watch your language! You're sentimentalizing and anthropomorphizing. You're casting perfectly lovely animals into your pathetic soap opera. Bad, bad!* (More on this later.)

Some of the more habituated sows do, in fact, place themselves near groups of people quite purposely. Call it babysitting, if you like, if you must use a metaphor. Big boars are a danger to cubs—something about getting them out of the way so the sows will go into estrus and satisfy their sexual desires—but generally keep their distance from humans. Mother bears have found that they can relax their guard as long as they stick close to people. They have even been known to run with their cubs to people when feeling threatened.

We didn't see that, but we did, another day, watch two bears have an altercation in which one ran away from the other—right to us. Guide Doug stepped in front and clapped his hands as the chased bear brushed past us and the chaser stopped short. The first hid behind us as though we were a barricade.

The guides, by the way, always carry shotguns. They are proud to say that, since human access has been limited at McNeil, no bears have been shot in the sanctuary. And no people have been hurt by bears.

๕

Did I mention that I was going to watch the bear watchers?

The truth is, they weren't nearly as interesting as the bears. Oh, there was the Italian bear biologist who had never seen a wild bear. (The park she worked in held a few of the rare European brown bears, but she had never seen one. I found that quite interesting.) There was the thirteen-year-old girl from Anchorage who let us all know, often, that she would have much preferred to be at the mall with her friends and who made her mother promise to take her for all-you-can-eat king crab as compensation for her exile. Annoying, not interesting. There was the hospital administrator and his teenage son with every bit of their outdoor clothing and camping gear, including mosquito-net hats, enviably new. There was another father and son who had the same first and last names—no nicknames—and I found myself wondering how they negotiated things like phone calls. There was Peggy from Texas, who really did have an article of clothing—a sweatshirt—with bears on it.

All of us wore hip boots for trekking across the flats and through the creek, but only Peggy got stuck in the mud and had to be lifted out of her boots. All of us had cameras and binoculars of varying commitment. I had my own camp chair that folded up to be carried in a bag over my shoulder like a yoga mat. All of us kept our stashes of food in the camp cookhouse and cooked separately on the propane burners there. In the field, we snacked on trail mix and beef jerky while we watched bears strip the skin off squirming salmon.

We were a chatty group. Bears would be walking by on our right and our left, and we would be turned to one another—*How do you like that new waterproof material?* and *I switched to digital, blah-blah-blah.* No one lowered his or her voice, but the bears didn't seem to care. They were habituated, after all, to our particular kind of verbal behavior. If they were the biologists and we were the subjects of their study, they might see that our inability to be quiet around one another is what makes us social animals. As social animals, we're able to strategize together about how to build subdivisions, play football, and attack other countries. Except when they gather to feed in these unusual situations like McNeil, bears much prefer to be loners—and thus come by their lower ranking in world dominance.

⁂

The bears didn't need to say a word to be, in my completely objective, journalistic, non-PETA opinion, endlessly fascinating.

Dolly was the female with two cubs who we saw most frequently. The three walked past us as they traveled between the top of the bluff, where they lay in a heap to nurse and snooze, and the creek, where Dolly stood attentively in the shallows and waited for a fish to bump into her legs while the cubs leaned against one another on the shore just behind her.

Dakota was the other female with a cub—the one that had done all that bawling my first day and that generally followed its mother like a caboose on a train.

Derek was a highly successful fishing bear, lunging again and again through the creek to come up with salmon flapping in his jaws—at least eight of them as we watched one afternoon.

Otto had a drooping lower jaw that made him look like a slack-mouthed idiot. The broken jaw, the guides said, was a not-uncommon injury among bears who sparred with their mouths open.

Luther was a huge, dark, low-slung bear—his frighteningly large private parts just about dragging—estimated at 1,200 pounds and likely, said the guides, to reach 1,500 pounds by summer's end. When Luther stepped up, every other bear got the hell out of the way.

Elvis shook his hips like you wouldn't believe.

We learned to recognize Dusty, Waterfallbear, Holden, Gash, and Reno. We watched male bears in pursuit of females (often seemingly reluctant), two bears nearly fall from a cliff while fighting, bears thrashing bushes, an almost-white bear, skinny bears, fat bears, a female with three cubs of very different sizes (one enormously porky), a bear with Mickey Mouse ears, a bear with white claws and another with a bent claw that made you think he would be cleaning his teeth with it, bears with very impressive scars, mellow bears and morose bears, annoyed jaw-popping bears, swimming bears, sleeping bears, pooping bears, bears employing every method of fishing you can imagine (short of using nets or poles), and bears flailing around most incompetently and never catching any fish.

One afternoon I looked around from where I was sitting and counted thirty bears. Most of them were fishing, a few were grazing, and two couples were working on creating next year's cubs while, in one case, a disappointed suitor watched from a half-lotus position. Dakota and her cub glided past, and—I couldn't help myself—I thought she was the most beautiful bear I'd ever seen, so beautiful that my heart skipped a beat.

I'd gone goofy over bears.

Here's my excuse: It's hard not to anthropomorphize animals, especially when you can tell one from another, and more especially when they have names. I came to McNeil thinking *sow* and *boar* and knowing that I was unsentimental about animals, and pretty soon I was thinking about *mama* and *sweet baby bear*, having a heartthrob for Dakota and a sad sorrow for the scrawny little fellow who couldn't seem to catch a fish. I began to interpret the moods of bears and to think about the ways they walked and sat and snuggled together in terms I would use for people. I said, right out loud, ridiculous things like, "Look how patient Dolly is. She's such a good mother."

We had a discussion one day about names. The McNeil biologists don't systematically name bears; it's just that, over the years, certain bears became familiar to them and, in order to talk about them, they had to say which bear they meant. "The female that we see a lot by the water-fall." "The really dark male with the scar on his side and another one under his eye." "The skinny sub-adult that belongs to the sow with the really big ears." It was a heck of a lot easier to just give them names.

The day of the discussion, guide Tom was in a bit of a quandary. The National Park Service people, who manage nearby lands and were part-nering in a remote-control camera to put McNeil bears at the fingertips of Internet users, wanted something for the Web site (http://magma .nationalgeographic.com/ngm/wildcamgrizzlies) to help viewers watch for particular bears that might appear at the falls. They'd asked Tom to give them a list of easily distinguished bears with names and photos.

Identifying bears that way, Tom thought, was unscientific, not worthy of an organization concerned not with individual celebrity bears but with bear research and management. A focus on named bears could lead people to think of bears as other than wild creatures.

I agreed with this.

But, others argued, what's wrong with people getting to recognize and appreciate a particular bear? That's the way to make them care, and once they care about bears they can name, they'll be more likely to support habitat protection and other good things. It's the old save-the-children syndrome; no one cares about abstract children, but they'll send money to mud-smeared Mia from Bolivia.

We all agreed with that, but wasn't that something an animal advocacy group should do—not a state agency that was supposed to be scientifically credible?

"What if," Tom said, "instead of saying 'This is Luther,' we say 'This is the bear we call Luther?'"

I was thinking of Treadwell again, and the names he'd given to the bears he considered his friends. He had chosen teddy-bear names—Tabitha (the name of his childhood teddy bear, which he had dragged along into real bear country), Mr. Chocolate, Sgt. Brown, Freckles, Downy, Booble, Ms. Goodbear, Cupcake, Aunt Melissa, The Grinch.

There were identifying names, and then there were names that truly defied the boundaries between humans and wild animals.

I would draw the line. I mean, *really*—show some respect!

🐾

All the mother-cub combinations we saw seemed to involve one-and-a-half-year-olds—little bears the size and rotundity of unshorn sheep. Where were the new cubs fresh out of their birth dens, the cubs of the year?

The "coys," guide Tom said, were simply few. The usual females—Dolly, my girl Dakota, and a few others who could hold their own in a crowd—had given birth the year before. Younger and less confident females with new cubs were, for safety's sake, likely keeping their distance from the bear throng. The only set the guides had seen frequented the beach area. "Keep an eye out there in the evening," Tom advised. "They sometimes come up into the sedge flat right below the camp."

That evening the triad did indeed appear just below the camp. The not-known-by-any-name mother bear was large and wooly looking, with an even tawniness to her coat and ears that shone yellow in the evening light, the same low light that filled the sedges and the rye grass and patches of beach greens with such radiant green glow. She waded slowly through the sedges, gripping and ripping, lowering her head and then raising it to chew and to glance, with ursine aloofness, at our little group of humans watching from the edge of the campground.

The two cubs, not much bigger than bread boxes and half hidden in the vegetation, kept close beside their mother. They were both a dark-chocolate brown, with the cream-colored "natal necklaces" that baby bears all come with—that make them look like they're wearing little sweaters. One kept standing on its hind legs, with front paws bent at chest level, to toddle around with remarkable balance. *Like a circus bear,* I thought, and immediately censored myself. *No! Not like an exploited animal meant to entertain me. Like a wild animal learning its way in the world and astonishing itself with every possibility.*

The same standing cub rested against its mother's high back, then pulled itself up into the saddle position behind her shoulder hump. Its sibling climbed up behind, and the two of them, balanced there, turned their little bear faces to watch us watching them. They lurched from side to side as their mother, wholly indifferent to us and our clicking cameras, worked her way back toward the gravel beach. The fecund smells of crushed vegetation filled the air, while an eagle eyed the whole scene from its driftwood perch on the beach and another, distant bear prowled the tide line. The rearmost baby bear at length slid off, tumbling little paws over little tush, and I heard myself saying, *aaaahhhh,* the way an old woman would gush over a baby in a bonnet.

I stood with my people, all of us, still talking, captivated by the baby bears. Oh, they were cute all right. There was no denying that the little bears in their little sweaters were very cute indeed. And we were only human—destined, perhaps, always to approach the rest of the world on our own terms and always to be a little silly about the things we fear and love.

IN OUR TIME

ONCE THERE HAD BEEN only the point of land and
the unnamed horseshoe-shaped lake surrounded by smaller
lakes and ponds and the wetlands between them. And the
woods, of course — the forest of dark spruce flowing back
to the glacier- and river-spilling mountains and forward to
the edge of the bluff, where eagles perched in their tops,
white heads like light bulbs. The horseshoe lake and surrounding lands, in our time first owned by the state of
Alaska and then by a Native corporation, felt like a secret
garden: hidden from the rest of the world, precious to
us. We set our Bird Dog down where other planes never
dared and kept it tied in the lily pads at one end of the
lake, where our trail began. A mile through the woods,
skirting beaver ponds and then the edge of the creek that
tumbled down to Cook Inlet's shore, brought us to our
summer fish camp.

On this August day, we circled over the point of land as Ken tested the winds and made sure the lake surface was clear of floating logs. Alert for wildlife, I spotted two black bears crossing a muskeg — a mother bear followed by its cub of the year. I looked down at the blue water of our lake and the next lake over — the one where Doris and Chet, before our time, had lived in a log cabin — and the pond above Fred's camp — the one his son drowned in, also before our time. I looked into the woods that I knew hid the depressions called "house pits" — where Dena'ina people, way before our time, lived in warm winter homes dug into the earth.

I tried very hard not to look at the dirt road that snaked around the lakes and over the high ground across the point and to the north. I tried not to see where a branch of it came right to the edge of our lake near the best berry bushes. I looked away from what was at the end of the road, above Fred's camp, just beside the pond — the enormous gravel pad laid out with a half-dozen bulk-storage oil tanks and several long, blue buildings fitted with chimney stacks, like some kind of grotesque crematorium.

We circled out over the edge of the bluff, over Fred's camp — his several small buildings bunched at the shoreline, boarded and lonely looking — and the water moving in along the sandbar. The salmon would be following the bar — were certainly flooding in with the tide, as they always have. I had a picture in my mind, of the commercial fishery in the 1930s and '40s, when the flats there were fished by dozens of fishermen all competing with one another, sometimes slashing one another's nets. Especially for king salmon, that sheltered bay on the south side of the point had been one of the hottest hot spots in all of Cook Inlet. On this day, there wasn't a fishing buoy to be seen, not there and not for miles around.

Just a mile out, lit and looming high over the water, the Osprey Platform — the inlet's newest — pumped oil out of the geologic depths and ashore. The crude filled the tanks and then was piped, through a line beside the road, to more oil facilities farther north.

The Bird Dog coasted in between dead standing trees and settled onto the lake. As we taxied toward the end, we took off our headsets and I shouted above the engine noise to tell Ken about seeing bears.

⚓

It had been several years since we'd really operated our fish camp — since we'd set out our nets each fishing period and sold our catch to tenders that made their way along our beach, stopping at each camp and then carrying the collected salmon across the inlet to the fish plants that processed them. The global competition with farmed salmon had sunk prices so low that the processors no longer found picking up our fish worth the fuel. There were plenty of salmon closer to the plants, salmon that could quickly be iced — another requirement if they were to compete for quality with farmed fish.

For a few years we'd continued to fish in a reduced way, catching a boatload on good-weather days and taking them across the inlet ourselves or paying our neighbor Fred to take our fish on a new boat he bought just for hauling. But then that wasn't worth the effort or risk. Our nets stayed in their covered totes, our skiffs onshore, and we used just one short net on a running line to catch the few salmon we wanted for ourselves — for our smokehouse and to carry home in our packs as fresh fillets. Then there were other things we needed to do in the summer, and we made the trip to camp less often, for shorter stays. Airplane maintenance kept the Bird Dog grounded for more than a year. We missed a whole summer.

We hadn't meant to give up fishing. We hadn't known we were giving it up. We were waiting for markets to adjust, for the tenders to come back, to figure out another way. The fishing life that we'd chosen in 1978 just slipped away. One by one, our fishing neighbors departed, leaving behind their boarded-up cabins and long stretches of open beach. The oil drilling platform arrived, and the onshore facilities to go with it.

Now we were back — too late for the red salmon, in time for the silvers that ran the beach. We came not to fish (except for what we could carry home to the freezer) but to give ourselves a few days at camp to do whatever needed to be done along with the things we missed so much — long beach walks, agate hunting, cutting firewood and then sitting by the woodstove "with our feet up on the oven door." We didn't literally put our feet on the oven door — our woodstove was just for heat and didn't have an oven — but we used the expression, one we'd adopted from our neighbor George and that invoked for us, as it had for him, the comfort of a warm cabin when the rain lashed down and the waves crashed on the shore.

At the lake we thrashed in the bushes until we found the tie-down to clip to the plane's tail. We slung on our packs and stepped around the rowboat, overturned on a couple of rotting logs. If we hadn't known where the trail was, we might not have found even its muddy beginning. We pushed through alders and the broad, spiny leaves of devil's club, into the woods.

For a decade, the woods had been apocalyptic, not-so-slowly turning from spruce forest to a landscape resembling the aftermath of a hurricane or bomb blast. Spruce bark beetles, which had first devastated the forests in our hometown and all across the Kenai Peninsula, had eventually crossed the inlet. We'd seen it all: clouds of flying insects, pinprick patterns in bark, sticky secretions of pitch (as trees tried to "pitch out" the invaders) and thick clusters of cones (as trees tried to maximally propagate before death), the red forest of the newly dead, the gray forest of the dead dead, the splintered forest.

Calling out to bears — a woods habit to keep from surprising any — we fought our way through the splintered forest. A dead spruce stays standing for a while, then dries to brittleness. For years already, every windstorm had snapped more trees, leaving ragged stumps and crisscrosses of fallen trees, with very few soldiers left standing. The forest had turned from vertical to horizontal.

In the old days, our trail maintenance consisted of swinging a machete a couple of times a summer as we passed through. In recent years we'd needed to cut our way clear with a chainsaw, repeatedly.

Once most of the spruces were down we thought we could get back to faster travel. What we hadn't anticipated was that the loss of sheltering spruce would cause a blowdown of exposed birch trees. Now we were blocked by gnarly old birches, some ripped out by their shallow roots, as well as shattered spruces. And while we'd been away the understory — false azalea bushes, prickly rose, the dreaded devil's club — had chased the light into every opening.

We would be back with the chainsaw from camp, but for now we had to zig and zag, climb and duck and fight our way through and around the wreckage. The trail itself was nearly obliterated, but we found the edge of the beaver pond and then a fern-filled area we recognized and some old cuts we'd made, and finally, after passing it and coming back, the top of the bluff where the creek started its fall.

"Where are you going?" I shouted to Ken, who was testing a log that lay across the first part of the creek's descent.

"It's more open this way," he called back.

"I'm staying on this side." I've never liked the tightrope act of log walking, and our regular trail, if I hit it, descended to the creek bed from its north side, where I already was.

Soon enough I was down the bluff to the logjam in the creek where our water system begins — where we place a bucket and start the long black piping that gravity-feeds our cabin. I waited there for Ken. I yelled and got no answer. I decided he was ahead of me and cursed him for not waiting. I ran down the rest of the trail, clear under overarching alders, until I was almost at the cabin, and stopped at a muddy spot. No tracks. I ran back up the trail and shouted for Ken some more.

I imagined Ken crumpled by a heart attack in the woods, being chewed by a bear, fallen with a broken leg. How would I ever find him? Why ever had we split up? I began to climb the hill on his side of the creek. I called again and heard only the crash of the creek.

This place that had always been so familiar suddenly felt threatening — and very lonely. Aside from whoever worked at the oil facilities up past the lake and the two separated-in-the-woods bunglers we had become, there were no other people for miles and miles around.

And then I remembered my phone. I dug in my pack for it, turned it on, and punched in Ken's number. It rang and rang and then he answered. "I'm just at the top of the bluff," he said, out of breath. "A little south of camp. I'm going to come down the bluff. It was all deadfall between me and the creek."

We met on the beach, and then we opened the cabin and took the shutters off the windows and found everything pretty much as we'd left it — camp shoes by the door, hats on the hooks, emptied kettle on the stove. The table, cluttered with reading material and agates, was gritty with fine sand blown in through cracks around the windows. Ken checked the batteries fed by our two solar panels. I picked up a *New Yorker*, open to the last page I'd read.

Before cell phones, our communications with the outside world depended upon a marine operator we might be lucky to raise on the VHF radio. Before that, we shouted "looking for a landline!" into a CB handset, usually without success. Cell-phone technology had certainly added a measure of safety to bush living, but as I looked out onto our rocky beach and the gray inlet beyond, I thought only of sand blowing through empty, silent cabins.

❦

First business at the cabin, after hooking up the water, was beating back the wildness. I used my weed whacker — not the gas-powered kind from suburbia, but a wavy-edged blade on a long wooden handle, swung like a golf club. I whacked at the grass and pushki — the hollow-stemmed cow parsnip — around the cabin and along the trail to the outhouse, and I grabbed and tore out a plague of new alders by their roots. I was, as never before, biotically ruthless.

I have never been good at attacking weeds or at any kind of landscape altering. At camp in the past, I've always been carefully selective — protecting the fireweed stalks, the raspberry canes, the watermelon-berry plants. I weed around my strawberries and hesitate even to cut runners. When taking down alders, I've always been the brake on Ken's ambition, always arguing to cut only what we needed for the smokehouse.

I remember as a very small child, on a hike with my parents, brushing carefully past the plants that bordered a trail and feeling pained as my parents' "waffle-stomper" boots ground seedlings into the dirt.

I voiced my disapproval when my mother broke off a branch, only to feel further defensive when she laughed and told me that widening the trail was a good thing. I had given considerable thought to the integrity of plants and to the process of their growth, which seemed slow enough then to me.

Such was the nature of my conservatism.

I was feeling now, though, like the victim in a horror film, surrounded by mutant or at least overpowering vegetation I needed to repel. For the first time in my life, I whacked indiscriminately, clearing the yard, the strawberry bed, the outhouse trail with a straight and wide corridor, felling the fireweed and the berry plants with the pushki and angelica, the wormwood, horsetail, ferns, grass, and dandelions. Ken cut the alders and willows that were crowding the cabin, and then we continued along the creek, opening the area to sky. I took my clippers and went on up the trail, cutting back alder branches and devil's club, all the way up the bluff.

There I was, at last reenacting something primal for humans — the compulsion to "tame" the wilderness, to dominate, to establish my own occupancy as foremost. It felt like an act of desperation, a panicked swipe at keeping our meager presence alive amidst so much change.

🌿

The next day, unusually warm for August, Ken and I set off along the beach. The tide had turned, and we walked at the wet edge of the inlet, watching for the shine of agates and racing each other to snatch them. I studied tracks of a black bear (distinguished from those of a small brown bear by its toe and claw marks) and a pile of bear scat (full of devil's-club berries and slimy greens.) There were fox tracks, too, and the faint prints and brush marks of a porcupine dragging its tail. Ken pointed out a huge rock that had fallen down the bluff, punching a trail behind it and bouncing onto the beach. The still-sandy rock had not yet been washed by a tide.

Our pleasure at being on the beach was tempered by our acute awareness of the change in our relationship to it, our estrangement. Once we'd known the beach by each of its fishing locations — its lines and buoys, the hidden rocks, the way the currents ran at different stages of tide. Here we caught a lot of fish, here a lot of sticks. Here was where the lead line always annoyingly caught in rocks, and here was where we came ashore when the wind blew from the southwest and the breakers were too big by our camp. Here was George's best net and where we'd pull alongside, bumping boats, to see how he was doing. Out there was where the cannery scow anchored, or the tender stopped; remember how slow our skiff was, full of fish and bucking the tide, how fast we'd fly back to nets "popping like popcorn" with more salmon?

The beach had lost its patterns and particularized meaning; it was now a long, bare stretch of rock and sand facing a blank expanse of water. The salmon were still out there, passing quietly, unimpeded. They would reach the rivers, to be flailed at by increasing mobs of sport fishermen.

I kicked at a piece of corroded metal pipe washed up on the gravel. I said to Ken, "How many people would recognize this as anything except trash?"

Ken stopped poking through the drift logs at the top of the beach. "Look at that," he said. "A stake."

In the old days, before our time, the fishermen along our beach used to tie their nets to such stakes, driven into the mud and clay. In more modern times, we hand-drilled a type of expanding bolt into rocks and tied to a metal eye. But every now and then at low water, when the beach sediments shifted, we'd find an old, rusting stake still sticking out of the mud, and we'd think about the fishermen who had been there before us. Who were they? How well had they done there, at that site?

We came to the place we know as Nick's, named for the fisherman who once, before our time, lived in the tiny cabin tucked into a break in the bluff. We've always stored our boats on the level ground there and stopped now to check them — the fiberglass skiff overturned against one hill, and the larger and heavier aluminum one pulled up in the tall grass and growing, when I checked it, a layer of moss. The cabin was where George's help usually stayed — for several years a couple we liked very much and then a long line of mostly young men. One of those young men had decorated by painting a dagger dripping blood on the door, and others spent their free time drinking and firing guns. The path was now completely overgrown with tall grass and nettles, and the sagging cabin looked decidedly derelict.

A little farther along Ken and I paused at a cluster of short posts — eight of them — sticking out of the sand. I tried to imagine what Stonehengian explanation a future archaeologist might give to them. Every spring a new young man had followed George's instructions to dig a very deep hole and plant a tall spruce pole, for tying a net at this location. Every winter ice sheared off the pole, leaving a rounded stump.

When we approached George's camp, with its red-and-white tarpaper siding, I half expected to spot some fluttering color and movement — George himself busy on the beach, mending a net or coiling lines or digging a new channel for his creek, any of the myriad camp projects that would typically have his attention. I recalled the September day in 1978 when Ken and I first walked from our newly purchased camp and saw smoke floating from the chimney. George stopped whatever he was doing and invited us into the warm kitchen, where he had us sign a guest book and his wife Charlotte served us hot chocolate. We heard the first of many stories we would eventually hear many times over, and when we left, George pressed a newspaper- and twine-wrapped package of smoked salmon into our hands and said, "Welcome to the beach."

Charlotte died from heart disease only a few years later, but every spring we again signed George's guest book and began another season of neighborliness. At George's table, we consumed stacks of sourdough waffles, played cards with visiting grandkids, and listened to George's stories about the days when his camp had been a cannery, when fishermen had fought over fishing sites, when he and his son Buck had hunted beluga whales. George was forever pulling from his many files old newspaper clippings and magazine articles he'd share with us, about bush pilots and trappers and people he'd once known to do extraordinary things, and about health remedies. He would jump up in the middle of a sentence if he saw his favorite eagle fly by, and run out to throw it a fish head.

The last time we'd seen George on the beach was the day he'd left, toward the end of the 2003 season, which wasn't a fishing season at all but, for George, another summer at his camp, his time filled with what we came to call "George projects." To fetch a cable he'd left at Nick's he'd need to fix the starter on his ancient beach buggy, but first he'd have to find a certain tool, which itself would need to be sharpened, but before he could do that he'd need to clear a space on the workbench, which involved moving things he had stacked there into a wooden box that had to have a slat replaced, and George would go off to find a piece of wood he could make into a slat. On that day, George's granddaughter was waiting for him on the other side of the inlet, and we helped him load his skiff. He hadn't quite finished closing up his camp, and we promised him, as we waved him off on the high tide, that we'd take care of the rest. We drained the plumbing, capped the chimney, boarded up the last windows, and locked the door behind us.

The next spring we visited George in the hospital. He survived a stroke only to die in June of a heart attack, age eighty-five.

Alders and willows were pressing in around the old cannery, and driftwood from the highest tides had lodged behind its front pilings. The big wooden dory that George built and used for so many years rested on the side dock, looking like a museum piece. Above the front, shuttered window, the swallow nest box was tipped to one side, as abandoned as the rest.

Ken and I circled the building, checking that windows and doors were still covered and locked. The place belonged now to someone from another state — Utah? — whom we'd never met. After George's death, his family had struggled to find a buyer for the property and fishing operation, for which, George used to brag, he'd turned down a million-dollar offer. They sold it for a pittance, the only value — and not much of that — adhering to the ten acres.

Bears had left paw marks on a high back window, which they'd reached by climbing up on the old cannery retort — the giant pressure canner. There was no sign that the new owner had visited. At least, I thought, a person exists who thinks he might want to spend some time here, sometime, or who perhaps speculates (even if only in the financial sense) that someone else might. That was better than the fate of so many other cabins all along the beach, sliding down hills or into the sea, sinking into the earth. The next cabin up the beach, moldering for years already at the spot we knew as Coal Gulch, had almost disappeared into the brush. A person passing on the water might not even spot it and certainly wouldn't guess at its colorful history: the seal hunter who built it, the family that overwintered and almost starved, the disagreement over ownership that had George going to court. The stories are fragments now, as fragile as anything made of wood.

I looked at the trees and the fireweed, the driftwood logs, the creek and the gravel berms — all that nature closing in around George's — and I wanted to fight back. I wanted to pull weeds and whack grass, to cut alders and clear out the pushki and the devil's club. I wanted to restore a sense of order and occupancy to my camp and to George's, to Fred's and Nick's and Coal Gulch and the rest, to all the lonesome places that were without their people. If I could beat back the encroaching chaos, maybe I could believe that all of us were gone just for the day — off delivering fish, or visiting another neighbor up or down the beach — and would be back.

This craving for human control of the land was shockingly new to me. I've always defended wild places and have wanted them to be kept in their wild perfection. This was different — a place not wild but storied, with a long human history about to be lost behind the trees and below the tides. In this place, humans have lived with salmon since the earliest times, since the Dena'ina people first came down out of the mountains to find an easier living along the shore. Who will love this place when we're gone? Who will know to watch the fireweed blossoms to announce the arrival of the red salmon, or will care that the salmon follow the beach and the bears walk the tide line? What does an emptied place, without its stories, mean to anyone — other than another piece of acreage to drill for oil or rip for coal?

I admit that I've always had a penchant for nostalgia, whether for woods and fields lost to paving and shopping malls or old cellar holes and bottle dumps hidden away in new woods. This is inconsistent, I know — this desire for both the unspoiled and the one-time despoiler — but I was the kid who wanted to be both a Lewis-and-Clark explorer and a Little-House-in-the-Big-Woods pioneer. It was a long time before I realized that the romance I attached to the homestead cabins I found rotting back to earth did not at all fit the difficulties and lost dreams of actual homesteading.

My feelings are complicated and personal. As we turned back from George's, I watched Ken, ahead of me, stoop with something less than nimbleness for another agate. We are mortal, yes, and one day, perhaps sooner than we might think, we, too, will leave the beach and not come back. My sadness was not so much for ourselves, or for the end of a phase of our individual lives, but for the break in a continuum that has gone on and on for so very long — this place and its people, with fish.

I took a last look at George's chimney and remembered the first time — how we were drawn by its column of smoke, eager to discover what we would find at its source and what kind of a life we might be entering as fishermen.

I understand the reasons — economic, social, technological — that have brought so much change. I understand that things are always changing. One of the first books I read when I moved to Alaska — and one I still return to — was Edward Hoagland's *Notes From the Century Before*, an elegiac portrayal of the old-timers in and around Telegraph Creek, British Columbia. I remember this from near the end: "Of course the future takes care of itself. All we know is what is lost, not what will be invented."

Who today really wants to fish on such a rocky beach, where you can't zip around on four-wheelers or use tractors to move your nets? Who wants to be without the option, at the end of a fishing day, of a long hot shower and a big greasy burger?

And yet I have this fantasy:

The deck shakes, and Ken and I look out, expecting a bear, but it's two young people who've walked from somewhere up or down the beach, where they're planning to fish. We serve hot chocolate and smoked salmon, show off our agate collection and some of the cedar corks from an old net we found eroding out of a bank near one of our sets. I get out our record books to see what we caught our first year, what prices were at their peak in '88, and when it was we switched from 25- to 40-horsepower outboards. Ken draws a map of the beach with its fishing locations and an illustration of a net rack, and he tells them how we used setlines strung between buoys, in our time. He advises them on their water system and goes to get them an extra bucket, left from the year we thought we could sell salted salmon. But to get to the stack of buckets behind the cabin he has to move the woodpile, and then he needs to cut away some alders, and then he has to search for the drill to make a hole in the bucket and then go under the cabin to take apart an unused part of our water system to get a hose clamp, which is rusty and has to be treated with rust remover. Ken and I laugh about his George project — and then we explain about George.

OUT AND BEYOND

The earth is what we all

have in common.

WENDELL BERRY

MAGADAN LUCK

MAGADAN OBLAST, a far-eastern stretch of the Russian Republic, lay beyond even Siberia. Despite its physical proximity to Alaska, in 1989 there was hardly a more exotic location on my map.

We met our Russian counterparts, scientists with the Institute of Biological Problems of the North, in Magadan, at the time a city only somewhat smaller than Anchorage. One studied the plankton in lakes, another the population cycles of lemmings, still others the successions and distributions of plants.

"And what is your specialty?" they asked.

Our interpreter helped me, saying, "She works for senators," which is what I'd been doing for the last decade — working as a legislative aide, mostly on resource issues, for the Alaska State Legislature during its winter sessions. The Russians only looked puzzled. I pantomimed catching fish with a rod and reel, then positioned my hands — fingers splayed — across one another to look like web.

"Ah! *Ribatchka!*" Our hosts' eyes lit up. We would go fishing!

※

In the late 1980s, when the "ice curtain" that had separated Alaska and Russia during the Cold War began to lift, opportunities for "friendship flights" and cultural exchanges came knocking. The idea behind our university-sponsored "expedition" of Alaskans to the Soviet Far East was that we would join with counterparts to work on biological or environmental problems. I'd envisioned something like hauling tires out of a trashed river, or planting seedlings in a deforested area. I was game for whatever they asked us to do. All I wanted was the entrance ticket to that mysterious northern land, that country that's been called Alaska's divided twin.

When I packed my duffel for Magadan, I threw in a light-weight spinning rod that had come in the mail one day, a bonus for buying a new outboard. Although I knew something about fish, I didn't often meet them on the end of a line. My idea of fishing was standing in a skiff knee-deep in sockeyes, snapping web from gill, the muscles in my hands aching. In my circles, to "fly fish" meant to load salmon into airplanes to be hauled to processors.

※

Thus it happened that I found myself with a dozen botanists and a black dog the size of a bear, hurtling through the sky in a giant Soviet helicopter, then landing on a sandbar and disembarking into clouds of mosquitoes. We had entered the Magadan Reserve, one in a system of natural areas set aside for preservation and scientific study. A broad, slow-moving river flowed through a landscape of stubby black spruce and birch forests leading into low, purple hills. Several small buildings — the reserve's headquarters, home to its guardian rangers — were half-hidden in the trees, just up from the riverbank.

There were more than enough hands to help with dinner, so I took my rod down to the river, tied on a Mepps lure, and made some casts. The river was too shallow adjacent to the sandbar, so I walked upstream to where the bank fell off more sharply. The mosquitoes weren't any worse than in interior Alaska, which is not to say that they weren't among the worst in the world.

Vladimir, one of our hosts from the institute, appeared on the bank, sucking on a cigarette. He spoke to me in Russian, none of which I understood, wrinkled his nose, waved derisively with his hand, pointed at my rod, frowned. Translation: This wasn't a good fishing place, and my equipment was totally unsuitable.

For dinner, served at an outdoor table balanced on logs, we had fish-head soup. Our uninitiated Americans gamely sipped broth from around the staring salmon eyes, the white globs of milt, and the legions of kamikaze mosquitoes that dove into their bowls.

After the hours-long dinner, after the speeches and toasts and the exhausting efforts at politeness and communication, I was ready for my sleeping bag. Our interpreter called me over. "You're going fishing," he said. Vladimir was nodding. So was a man who looked like he'd just stepped out of a jungle; he was wearing a mosquito-net hat with the net tied up away from his face, a dirt-colored heavy-duty field suit with a huge knife on the belt, and several days' beard. This was Boris, assistant ranger. Boris pointed downriver. Just over there, we would go, just for a little while, we would definitely catch some fish.

I didn't seem to have a choice. I recruited Debby, one of our botanists, and we zoomed off in a powerboat with Boris and Vladimir.

That far north, early in July, there was plenty of light at ten thirty. The sky was stretched with cirrus clouds, high and feathery and lit from below with pale pink edges. The river washed past snags of fallen trees and banks overgrown with grasses. Debby peered into the foliage, recognizing a lupine, a spirea. We rounded one bend and another and then pulled up beside a side slough.

Fish waggled in the bottom of the pool. I hadn't known what we were to fish for, but I recognized these by their sail-sized dorsals. We traded our names for them — *kharioos*, "grayling" — as we readied our poles. Vladimir had a spinning rod with a big, shiny spoon. Boris brandished the world's largest fly rod, nearly as thick at its base as my wrist, long enough to reach across the slough. Boris looked at my rod and, grimacing, said something to Vladimir. Whatever it was, it wasn't complimentary.

From the bank, I cast into the pool. On my second cast, a fish swept forward and took the lure.

Boris leaned his own pole into the bushes and ran to help me. Shouting excitedly, he grabbed my line and began to pull it in, fast, hand over hand. Debby and I looked at each other. "Must be the Russian way," I said. Boris yanked the fish up onto the bank, unhooked, it, and slid a stringer through its gills. It was a nice fish, perhaps fifteen inches long, its scales like rows of silver buttons. We all enthused over it, and Boris and Vladimir took up their poles again with a new intensity. I handed mine to Debby.

Debby caught a fish, and then I hooked one. Debby yelled, "*Nyet! Nyet!*" and wouldn't let Boris grab the line. "*Americanski* way," we told him and showed what it was like to let the fish take off, to dive and fight and flash and be reeled back in. Boris looked worried and then amazed when I landed the played-out fish on my own. He stretched his rod across the slough and dropped his fly near the opposite bank. Vladimir, farther along, cast and cast again; his reel zinged as he cranked the line in.

Debby caught another.

Boris suddenly became very interested in my rod. He ran his hand over it, testing the flex, pinching the line. He held the lure in the air and let it twist, glinting, back and forth. He mumbled in Russian. "Try it," I said, pushing the rod at him, but he wouldn't take it.

"Vladimir," I said, "try this." I gave him one of my Mepps. He put it in his tackle box. I gave Boris a Mepps, too, and he dropped it into a jar with his homemade flies.

I cast again, caught and played and landed another grayling.

The men exchanged looks. Neither had hooked anything yet.

The sound of another boat whined toward us. It was Sergei, the head ranger, and two others of our party, fresh from the sauna. They admired our catch as we all swatted mosquitoes. Boris began to take his pole apart. He had an idea. He was going to get his net.

While he zipped back to the camp, the rest of us took the other boat around a couple more curves, to the river's juncture with a side creek. In the creek mouth, we could see where salmon-sized fish were finning, breaking the water into silvery rifts that reflected the remaining light. I flung my lure at them a few times, but it was too dark to hope for more than an accidental snagging. Sergei boiled water on a camp stove and served jam "tea" — a spoonful of jam stirred into a mug of hot water.

Boris returned with a pile of tangled gill net. I helped him work through the net, laying it out on the boat's bow — the line with cork floats to one side, the line with metal rings to the other, the web picked free of sticks in the center. "I do this in Alaska," I said. "Five species" — I held up five fingers — "in Alaska."

"*Keta*," Boris said, and I understood. The chum or dog salmon, the one with striped sides — its scientific name is *keta*. I spread my fingers again and made vertical stripes in the air. Boris grinned. We were talking about the same fish.

When the net was laid out neatly, we tied one end to shore where the creek merged with the river's slower water. We pushed the boat backward into the current with an oar, and the net spilled off the bow to lie in a line. We waited, and Boris described what a big splash we would see when a fish hit the net. The fish, though, weren't moving, or they weren't crossing the current, and so we left the net and motored back to camp.

In the morning, we had five *keta* salmon to add to our mess of grayling. Vladimir and I cleaned them. He used my dictionary to tell me that he respected a woman who cleaned fish.

❧

Later that week, I left the botanists and joined another group of Alaskans to fly a thousand miles to the Arctic, to a research station on the coastal plain. The scientists there specialized in parasites. None of us knew anything about parasites, but we were happy to go mountain hiking, set vole traps on the tundra, and eat reindeer stew. One day we boarded three powerboats and headed upriver, startling moose, reindeer, swans, geese, loons, hares — a richer collection of animals than I'd ever seen in one place. Our hosts were taking us fishing.

We wound back and forth along the ribbon of river. The mountain we'd climbed a couple days before was sometimes in front of us, sometimes to our right, sometimes behind us. Now and then the lead boat missed the channel and ground up a cloud of river bottom with its prop. I watched the banks; where the river cut into them, it exposed a wall of ice beneath the sod. I was hoping to spot a tusk or a frozen, fleshy leg of a mammoth. In the geological museum in Magadan, we'd seen a cast of a whole baby mammoth that had been found in similar permafrost.

Someone pointed. A leggy, flag-tailed, blond and copper-colored fox was racing along the shore. For a few seconds, it seemed as though the animal and we were part of the same stopped action, and that the backdrop land was what was moving past us. And then the fox was up over the bank and gone,

There were buildings ahead, wooden skiffs pulled up on the beach. We slowed and turned in. A couple of men came out of one of the cabins and watched us from behind a length of gill net that was hung, like a fence, in front of the camp. Wooden barrels were piled to one side.

I reached for my fishing pole, but Valeriy, the chief Soviet parasitologist, stopped me. Not yet. This was, apparently, just a social stop. Wilhelm, one of our drivers, knew the men here. They were preparing for the run of arctic char that would come later in the summer.

The men were dark, chain-smoking, and shy. Wilhelm talked to them while the rest of us stood around awkwardly. I looked into a barrel. It was stuck with lumpy gray salt and smelled like fish. I looked at the gill net, fingering the web, lifting the lead line. I assumed the net was stretched out for mending, which it needed, but I couldn't find where it had been mended, ever, nor any sign of needle and twine.

The men — Americans, too — had disappeared into one of the cabins.

I found them passing around and admiring hunting rifles. A pile of loose bullets lay on the nearest bed, sunk into the folds of a faded blue sleeping bag. An electric light bulb dangled from the center of the ceiling, and the most prominent object in the room was a large television set. I had to look longer to find the net-mending needle, burnished wood, . on a nail by the door. In Alaska our needles are made from plastic, and a wooden one would be in a museum.

It was time to go. We piled back into the boats and continued upriver, running aground with greater frequency, until we came to a wide curve in the river, a long gravelly beach where we anchored.

The morning's clouds had broken up into scraps of gray fleece, uncovering an ice-blue sky. The sun was almost directly overhead, and there was no shade anywhere. Valeriy pointed at the portion of river that swept around the curve, indicating that was where we should fish, but the water there looked too fast to me. I took my rod and cut across the top of the beach, through a sandy area where patches of dwarf fireweed were so thick with pink-purple blossoms they looked like bouquets stuck in the sand. I brushed past willow bushes, setting loose an air show of white fluff. The bank on the far side fell off sharply into a deep pool.

Kharioos. I could see half a dozen grayling, all good-sized, all lying on the bottom against the shore. They were finning as though fanning themselves, using as little energy as possible. Clearly, they were not in a mood for feeding.

I cast across the pool and watched my Mepps flash its way back, looking like nothing that might occur naturally in the river. It nearly dragged into one fish, which turned to look at it and then slowly eased back into position.

I fished for an hour like that, annoying one fish and then another, but never enough to coax any into a hit.

To tell the truth, I didn't mind about the fish. I felt the sun on my face and the Arctic breeze, and I listened to the water. I cast and cast again, and it was the motion that mattered — mindless, repetitive, rhythmic. I thought about Norman Maclean, the fisherman-writer whose father had used a metronome to teach him to cast, to melt into the rhythms of the universe.

My mosquito lotion wore off all at once, and, until I stopped to slather more on, I understood the panic of Alaska's caribou and Russia's reindeer, animals that sometimes get driven by mosquitoes to exhausted deaths. Back down the river, I could see the others, spaced apart, casting into faster water, Valeriy with a thick wool hat piled on this head like a turban. I mentally pinched myself. I was in the Soviet Arctic, fishing with Russians for Russian fish. How could I ever have imagined, growing up through all those years of anticommunism and Cold War fear, that this was possible? Here we were, Russians and Americans together, sharing the same universal rhythms, in what must be one of the wildest and most sparely beautiful — not to mention peaceful — places on our shrinking earth.

I worked my way toward the others, testing the fast water. When I reached Valeriy, he told me in his fractured English that he liked that I liked to fish and that he was impressed with American women. We — the three visiting at Ust-Chaun — were the first he'd ever met. I understood him to say that we did everything that Soviet women did and more, and I was embarrassed. I didn't think Soviet women had time for such idleness as fishing; they were all too busy, working double duty at their paid jobs and their domestic ones — the long hours of shopping for short supplies, preparing meals from scratch, homemaking without the labor-saving equipment Americans take for granted. Even at Ust-Chaun, among scientists posted to a remote research station, women were the ones cooking, caring for children, attending to chores.

At that moment, from a clearing near where the boats were anchored, Luda called us to tea. She had spread a picnic cloth on the ground and was slicing cucumbers. I carved a loaf of bread on our boat bow. The others trailed in. No one had caught any fish, no one complained, everyone plucked parboiled mosquitoes from their cups of tea. I practiced my Russian. *Komar*. Mosquito. Across the river a swan, its wings walloping the air with a sound like towels being snapped in the wind, launched itself, circled over us, and headed east.

We went back to fish some more. Luda stayed by the boats; she did not care to fish, she said.

The sun had fallen considerably, and I saw as I approached my fishing hole that it was now partially shaded by the bank. I heard the fish before I even came around the corner. They were rising though the shade, snatching at mosquitoes, leaving widening rings that merged one into another. They weren't jumping, just snouting through the surface, then falling back again. I cast into the pool, repeatedly. Now and then, a fish would make a run at my lure before veering off. I thought of Boris, back at Magadan Reserve, how much he'd love to be with us with his giant fly rod. When we left the reserve, I'd told him that when he came to Alaska, I would be *his* fishing guide. It had been the wrong thing to say, of course. We both knew his chances of ever coming to Alaska were close to zero. His chances of ever dropping a line in his own Arctic were probably similar.

And I thought again what I had thought a thousand times since arriving in the Magadan region: what right do Americans have, by the accident of their birth on one soil instead of another, to such enormous privilege?

I thought this like a mantra — what right, what right — and I listened to the river. Along the shore, it made a whispery noise, like rough cotton rubbing against itself. Farther out, it rustled around rocks with a silkier sound. After a while, I could hear single pieces of gravel washing past each other, but I still had no answer to my question.

By then I had sufficiently annoyed the pool of fish that one retaliated by striking my lure. We struggled with one another, back and forth along the bank, until I landed it, gills heaving, in the sand. I fished some more, and I had another. I hooked another and lost it. I caught a third, one so small I would have released it had I not hooked it so well.

I saw Wilhelm crossing a channel farther upstream, and then the others, everyone circling back to the boats. It was all I could do to break away, to reel in and not to cast again, to pick up my fish and leave my piece of river.

Back at the boats, we showed off our fish. With three, I was the high-liner again. Wilhelm, fly fishing, had caught only one. He flashed a huge, gold-toothed smile at me.

"You are happy," Luda said to me.

Yes, I was, and I also knew that was not exactly what she'd meant to say. The Russian language, I had learned, has a single word for both happiness and luck. If you're lucky, you must also be happy. If you're happy, it's not that you have some constitutional guarantee, some inalienable right to be so, but only that you have enjoyed good luck.

I looked up. I looked around me. I looked at my new friends. I couldn't speak any of what I felt, so I said the only word I knew that seemed to apply. "*Ochen*," I said. Very.

THE RINGS

IN WYOMING, I WALKED up a red-dust road, along a truck track, finally over the top of a mesa to a bench of land that looked down on a creek and across a valley to the snowy Big Horn Mountains.

And there they were, what I had come to see. An obviously human construct, the rings lay in short-cropped grass, among fragrant sage plants and many cow pies. I had expected, somehow, larger and fewer rocks, something less defined. What I found was more like solid low walls formed of many rocks, none bigger than footballs, laid end to end and side to side and embedded in the earth. For the most part, only their round, licheny tops were exposed. The rocks were gray and orange, different kinds and textures, and the lichens grown over them were green and brown and bright yellow. Anthills piled fine sand between and over some; others had been overturned, presumably by tripping cattle.

At home in Alaska, I was accustomed to coming upon rectangular holes in the ground, the shapes that record the dug-into-the-earth winter homes of our first people. Tepee rings, circles of rocks believed to have anchored the tepees of the Plains Indians, I found to be much the same sobering evidence. People lived in North America, not so long ago, in ways that were close to the earth and, quite literally, part of the earth. The old arrangements of earth and stone are fundamentally different from the civilizing artifacts we white people forced down on the continent. And they are scattered, lonely reminders of cultures that were, so recently, so vibrantly alive.

I strode across one circle, pacing it to twelve feet. A few more stones lay at its center. Was this the hearth of the home that was here? The word *hearth*, I reflected, contains both *heart* and *earth*.

Once, I nearly lived in a tepee. Years ago, when Ken and I were new to Alaska and in need of a place to live, I read an entire book about tepees, learning their history and styles, ways to adjust for weather and smoke, motifs for their exterior designs, pointers on arranging the living space. We got as far as ordering a canvas tepee, complete with lining and assembly directions, and cutting its black-spruce poles. But then, an actual house — with square corners, solid roof, electric heat — presented itself, and we took the easier path. We sold the tepee without even unpacking it. I've always regretted, to some degree, that lost opportunity to have lived, at least for a time, another kind of life. I could have done it then, when I was young and enthralled with possibility, still willing to live a different reality.

In Wyoming, I sat within that tepee ring, one of half a dozen crowded on that benchland, and thought about the ways we Americans romanticize the past, particularly that of the Native cultures we destroyed, the garden that once was. Hardheaded and unsentimental, I'm not one to go around burning sage or sprinkling corn in imitation of someone else's sacred ceremonies. I know what I am not. But I also remember something that Barry Lopez once said: that we don't need to be a people to learn from them.

And I am woefully ignorant. I know something of our shameful history, the cheating and massacring and dispossessing of the people who lived first on this continent. I know what sympathizer George Bird Grinnell, a collector of Indian lore, wrote after following the destruction of cultures all the way to Alaska in 1899: "There is an inevitable conflict between civilization and savagery, and wherever the two touch each other, the weaker people must be destroyed." But I also know what Grinnell didn't know in his time: that there are no savage, weak, or primitive cultures. There are only different cultures, grown up in different places and circumstances, wise in different ways. Indigenous cultures belong to places the way indigenous plants and animals do. Which doesn't mean that alien species — here tumbleweed and domestic sheep, for example — can't be introduced, can't prosper and squeeze out native species through competition, disease, their own adaptation. Horses came to America with the Spanish, and the Indians took advantage of what they offered, a new technology for getting around and chasing down game. White people brought muskets and gunpowder, smallpox, barbed wire; they brought the strength of numbers and organization, and they overtook.

I know these few things, but I don't even know which Native Americans — Crow, Shoshone, Cheyenne, Arapaho, or Sioux — camped there on the tepee hill. I don't know when they placed those rocks. Local people — the nearby museum director and librarian — could offer little information. All that's sure is that, before whites arrived to wrest the land away, people of many tribes came and went through the open country, living and warring and following the herds and the rain. The one location I explored seems ideal: the level, large-enough ground, the nearness of water, the gracious valley with its trafficking animals, a hawk's-eye view of it all.

What I saw when I looked out along the cottonwood-shaded creek were ranch-style homes with mown lawns and satellite dishes. Beyond them, the highway to Sheridan. A valley divided by fence lines separating fields full of black cattle and irrigation equipment. Red-tipped hills and, farther off, mountains still locked in winter. From my height I glimpsed what is only more obvious from jets passing overhead — a whole country marked off into grids and patchworks: summer and winter ranges, hay and alfalfa fields, homesteads and road crossings, the rare patches of high-elevation wilderness.

When the stone circles held down the edges of windblown tepees, there were no highways or fences, no black cattle. Instead, down in the valley, some of the Great Plains' seventy million buffalo roamed. Wolves chased the buffalo, and the great grizzly bears scavenged. Men, too, chased the buffalo; livings and lives were made here, from meat, robes, bones, and buffalo chips for fuel. The rigged-out, painted tepees, each constructed from a dozen buffalo hides, were set up and maintained by skillful women; as necessary, they were struck and dragged off on their poles to different ground. Once the land went on forever, rich in a way it will never be again.

The only buffalo near those rings today are fenced within a ranch that caters to tourists, who ride around in buses to feed the begging animals and are encouraged to kiss them on their rubbery noses. Ranch visitors are invited to purchase buffalo keepsakes including hides (tanned or green), skulls (plain or painted), meat (cured or fresh), horns, teeth, and buffalo breakfast sausage, not to mention buffalo videos, postcards, stuffed animals, and T-shirts. They can also eat at the buffalo steak and burger restaurant. The ranch's former star buffalo, named Tiny ("weighs as much as the entire L.A. Rams football team!"), was trucked to the state fair, where the confinement and noisy attention were apparently more than it could tolerate. It collapsed and died, a symbol I think for *something*.

At the tepee rings, the wind blew as it always has, hard out of the mountains. It caught my baseball cap and sent it flying over sage and cacti and the first blue flames of summer flowers. I understood why the people, in their buffalo-hide homes, around their cooking fires, needed to anchor themselves within solid circles of rocks. I was left thinking of all those buffalo, gone, and the Buffalo People with them, and the prairie grasses, the unfenced space, other ways of being and knowing. The rocks remain in their circles, hard evidence of what we've lost, of what we still stand to lose.

ENCOUNTERS WITH THE
OLD NATURALIST

IN WEST PARK, NEW YORK, at the top of steep Burroughs Drive, my friends and I parked at a gate before a dirt lane carpeted with September's leaves. The sign on the gate welcomed us to the property of John O'Bird.

I showed off my learnedness to David and Irene. "Muir was John O'Mountains. So Burroughs became O'Bird." "The two Johns," people called them — two bearded celebrants of nature. Muir was the Scotsman, although Burroughs was commonly confused as one. The Burroughs family, American farmers for generations, actually traced their ancestry back to Wales and Ireland.

Crunching over the leaves, along a path that seemed seldom traveled, we entered the John Burroughs Sanctuary. *Please leave the wildlife wild*, the hand-painted sign read.

David was being his usual truculent self. "As opposed

to what? Taking home a couple of deer to put in your garden?"

Wildlife, I might have pointed out, didn't have to be mammalian megafauna. Wildlife could be a beetle, a newt, the egg case on the underside of a leaf, the leaf itself. This was something David would know if he had been a student of Burroughs, if he had read the old naturalist's essays and appreciated the way Burroughs looked at all of nature as if under a microscope. I ignored David and thought instead about Burroughs's guests who had trod the road before us. By the time Burroughs had built Slabsides, his rustic cabin in the woods, his friends included many of the rich and famous. Henry Ford, Thomas Edison, Harvey Firestone — these all spent some deliciously nonmotorized and nonelectric days at Slabsides. Theodore Roosevelt, who dedicated one of his outdoor books to Burroughs with the inscription, "It is a good thing for people that you have lived," visited. John Muir came, always to badger Burroughs about what he considered his bovine contentedness and his friendships with men of position, who Muir thought should apply their wealth and power to conservation causes.

What an odd fellowship: the gentle nature writer, so concerned with following bees through the woods and determining the turning direction of bean and bittersweet vines, and the men of progress, self-promotion, and political cause. Muir would be swinging from trees while Burroughs rested blissfully on a pasture rock. Ford gave Burroughs a car, but Burroughs never got the hang of parking it in a barn without running into the back wall. In 1903 President Roosevelt, with his missus, walked the whole mile from the Hudson on a hot day.

Burroughs's own missus, Ursula, once wondered aloud why her husband was so popular. "They don't know you like I do," she said.

> On the steep, bushy mountain-side near the wharf [at Skagway] I heard the melodious note of my first Alaska hermit thrush. It was sweet and pleasing, but not so prolonged and powerful as the song of our hermit.

"In Green Alaska," 1901

The John Burroughs I knew best was the writer I'd met in another, distant context. In 1899, three years after he built Slabsides, Burroughs came to Alaska as part of the Harriman Alaska Expedition, a sightseeing and scientific survey cruise. He was sixty-two years old, at a time in his life when he admitted he wanted "less and not more." The report he left of the two-month expedition along Alaska's coast is, to me, frustratingly constrained by his inability to bring his — as he put it — "eye to the Alaskan scale." Alaska was too grand for him, too big and wild and foreign, and so he settled on filling his account with commentary on birds and wildflowers, especially the ones he rejoiced at recognizing from home.

A century after his Harriman journey, I used his account to trace my own path along Alaska's shores for a book I titled, in homage to his report, *Green Alaska*. Burroughs became for me the principal character to lead the way through the Harriman experience and to inform my own. I came to think of him as a kindly mentor, a guide to, if not Alaska, a way of seeing the natural world.

Now, I'd come from Alaska to Burroughs's own place to try to see if I could bring my eye to what he loved as passionately as I loved the north. I'd come to do my wondering about his near-disappearance from our literary map in the place where he'd made his reputation, and to decide for myself whether he — so out of fashion in our modern world — might still be worth hearing from.

> To a countryman like myself, not born to a great river or an extensive water-view, these things, I think, grow wearisome after a time. He becomes surfeited with a beauty that is alien to him. He longs for something more homely, private, and secluded. Scenery may be too fine or too grand and imposing for one's daily and hourly view. It tires after a while. It demands a mood that comes to you only at intervals. Hence it is never wise to build your house on the most ambitious spot in the landscape. Rather seek out a more humble and secluded nook or corner, which you can fill and warm with your domestic and home instincts and affections.
>
> "Wild Life About My Cabin," 1898

And there it was, emerging from the trees. Slabsides.

The setting was, well — neither fine nor grand. The cabin sat in a low spot — a swamp is what Burroughs called it. There were trees and bushes pressing in on all sides, some rock outcroppings, a wet hollow that even in the current drought held the kind of standing water mosquitoes love. Burroughs had raised his commercial crop of celery there. Through trees on one side we could just make out a ridge with more rock outcroppings. Somewhere there lay Julian's Rock, named for his son, who found the home site when wandering old wood roads one day, and where Burroughs liked to climb to look to farther-off mountains, the Shawangunks and the Catskills, as well as down upon his sheltered space.

Irene set up her tripod to photograph the cabin, which is, in fact, made up of slab sides, the rounded and barked sides of logs that are the first removed when trees are milled into lumber, and which Burroughs likened to the crusts cut from bread. The effect was lovely — the various colors of bark, from very dark to almost white, textured. The porch supports and railings were made of more logs and latticework of curved branches — the rustic "twig architecture" I'd noticed elsewhere through that mountain country.

On the porch, I peered through grill-covered windows. The cabin door was locked, but a notice posted beside it invited visitors to Slabsides Day, just a few days off, featuring a tour of the cabin, a guided nature walk, and a panel discussion presented by "five Burroughs enthusiasts." I wondered what Burroughs would think, about such fuss being made over him, and about the country that now surrounded us. Way back when his son was born, he'd lamented the "faded and dilapidated inheritance he has come into possession of." America, even then, was too modern for him, too removed from his ideal woods-and-farm-fields state.

A map of the area, posted in the window, was dated twenty years before. Another yellowed sheet, typewritten on a manual machine, told us that, during Burroughs's lifetime, "Slabsides was the most frequently visited literary shrine in America."

While I pressed my face to windows and Irene photographed, David read aloud from a guest book he found in a wooden box in the yard.

"This is a genuine American sacred site. . . . Burroughs was one of the great roots of my joyous ecological worldview along with Emerson, Thoreau, Melville, Dickinson, and Whitman."

"I have traveled from Seattle. I am on a mission to visit all of my favorite authors. . . ."

"I was led to this place by my guide, I believe. . . ."

Four children had come with a grandmother, and while present read aloud from "a book about Burroughs" they'd borrowed from the local library. Someone else, who wrote "kool dewd" (presumably a commentary about Burroughs), was linked by an arrow to another signature and the title "parole officer."

The most recent visitor, three days earlier, had listed what he'd found at Slabsides (chickadee, blue jay, nuthatch, several species of warblers, "and the tranquility of Wake-Robin"). *Wake-Robin*, long out of print, was Burroughs's first and best-known collection of nature essays, much about birds — although the title belongs to a plant (*Trillium erectum*, a spring-flowering perennial).

The cabin's interior was dark and dim, but Burroughs's writing desk sat just within one of the porch windows as though he'd only just left it for a walk in the woods. His tools were laid out: partly burned candle in a candlestick, blotter, pencils, wooden ruler, a huge brown book I knew from my reading to be Burroughs's much-turned-to dictionary.

Inside as outside, the interior walls and room dividers were built of more logs and poles, and the cabinets, tables, and stools — Burroughs's own "stick" constructions — bore elegant curves and knotty bumps. A rocking chair faced the stone fireplace, past a pair of tables set for dining, and a narrow birch bed on the far side was made up with linens and blankets. I could just make out what appeared to be banners hanging on the walls. Oh, yes, those college girls who flocked to Slabsides to picnic and take their nature lessons, to hear "Uncle" John's stories of his time in Alaska and admire his collections of twisted sticks and birds' nests.

The porch creaked under my feet, and I tried to sort out the melancholy that seemed to have descended upon me. I didn't feel like a pilgrim, come to worship at a shrine. I felt, instead, as though my friends and I had stepped into a freeze-frame — not of Burroughs's own time, but later, when his Slabsides was a more active memorial to the man, when his work was still read by ordinary, nature-gladdened people. The sad things were not the dusty writing desk and empty rocker but the aged notices, the signs of neglect that, despite the occasional message in the guest book and the approaching Slabsides Day, suggested that, really, what we had before us was — to use Burroughs's own words in another context — "faded and dilapidated."

David asked, "Was he really any good, or did he just hit on a good thing and keep churning it out?"

It was an honest question. Yes, Burroughs churned. I'd read enough of his writing to know that much of it was unexceptional. Anyone who wrote thirty books was bound to repeat himself, bound to be less than consistently brilliant. Burroughs could be too cute at times, or provincial and judgmental, or simply dull, and his writings had not all aged equally well. But give him credit; he inspired millions of readers to go out and meet nature firsthand. He could spin prose into beautiful form and sow wonder across the land, not every time but enough. David and I, both writers, could only dream of achieving Burroughs's popularity, of having our work adopted in classrooms across the country the way his had been. "I don't think we should be hypercritical just because he was both prolific and popular," I said. "He was original — no one else was writing from that kind of grounding in nature, and doing it with style."

One day a lot of Vassar girls came to visit me, and I led them out to the little sassafras to see the chickadees' nest. The sitting bird kept her place as head after head, with its nodding plumes and millinery, appeared about the opening to her chamber, and a pair of inquisitive eyes peered down upon her. But I saw that she was getting ready to play her little trick to frighten them away. Presently I heard a faint explosion at the bottom of the cavity, when the peeping girl jerked her head quickly back, with the exclamation, "Why, it spit at me!" The trick of the bird on such occasions is apparently to draw in its breath till its form perceptibly swells, and then give forth a quick, explosive sound like an escaping jet of steam.

"Wild Life About My Cabin"

I had no idea what a sassafras tree looked like. And, for all the chicka-dees I'd watched *dee-dee*ing their way through various woods, I've never seen a single one of their nests. I had not the attentiveness of the old naturalist, who would not have spotted a bird without following it to its roost and analyzing every aspect of its behavior. Burroughs had done this, as well, with bees, tracking them to their honey trees, and with chipmunks, calculating their winter stores. That was his gift: the child's sense of wonder that never left him, the curiosity about all living things, the ability to set the experience down so that readers, anywhere, might feel that they, too, had stuck their heads into trees. And were glad they had.

I walked behind the cabin and to the spring and the edge of the grown-over celery field, aware how little sight I brought to any of what I found myself among. I recognized some of the hardwood trees — maple, beech, oak — from the shapes of their just-falling leaves. Goldenrod was still golden, and the crumpling leaves of sumac blazed red. Crickets chirped, and the air carried a fragrance of leaf rot and wood smoke. Although I retain a modest memory of eastern woods from my growing-up years, this landscape wasn't home to me, and I didn't know how the maple tree related to the ferns at its base or the tiny critters that hid among the old leaves.

"I want to find Julian's Rock," I called. I had with me a picture of it, of Burroughs sitting on it, on the ridge above, and looking down on Slabsides.

Irene and David joined me to clamber up the hillside, so much more wooded now than in Burroughs's day. Most of the trees were hemlock and oak up to a foot thick, with rock outcrops but little brush among them. We found ledges and rock prongs that looked like good sitting sites, but the trees kept us from any view of the cabin. We couldn't find a top to the ridge or any openings to look down from, but we did spot some neighboring houses and worried about stumbling onto their properties, creating enmity for poor John Burroughs.

When we reached what seemed to be a public road, we followed it back to our car. Forest squeezed against the road, and I wondered aloud how much more "wild" the region was than it had been in Burroughs's day; so much of the country that had once been cleared for farming had returned to woods. I imagined that Burroughs would be surprised at such a "backward" turn. In his day, the litter of the bark peelers, who'd stripped every hemlock in sight for leather tanning, lay all around, and the nests of passenger pigeons, that had in his boyhood filled so many trees, were gone with the birds. The threats now were different, less easily laid at the feet of individuals. Coal-fired power plants and vehicle emissions, far to the west, were responsible for the sulfur dioxides and nitrogen oxides acidifying lakes and leaching away soil nutrients. Twenty percent of the lakes within Adirondack State Park, to our north, were so acidified that they no longer supported aquatic life, and acidic clouds had wiped red spruce off mountaintops.

We passed the open door of an artist's studio where a woman with her back to us brushed bright paint across a canvas. We passed another woodsy home with a fire burning in a pit out front and melted candles spaced along a fence. Burroughs, visiting Alaska, had referred to himself as a dreamer. Here, in his home place, among the sheltering rock ledges and woods, dreamers were still finding spiritual support and inspiration. I thought, *I could live here.* I could live with that smell of earth and fire, under trees. I could watch for the first trilliums of the year, for the wood warblers and the fox, and for the chickadee in its nest. I could learn, beyond telling a spruce from a hemlock from a balsam fir, what each needs to prosper.

> At Woodchuck Lodge the woodchucks eat up my peas and melons and dig under the foundations of my house.
> "Nature Lore," 1918

Another day, another drive. My friends and I pulled up to the summer home that Burroughs kept in his later years, on his family property in the Catskills. At Woodstock Lodge he is said to have composed some of his best-known essays from a straight-backed chair on the porch. The wood building, a registered national historic landmark since 1963, was boarded up and falling down. Upstairs shutters with moon cutouts blew back and forth in the wind, and the porch, with its rustic stick railings and a shelf holding a collection of bird nests, was soft and spongy underfoot.

Another guest book — and all the remarks were variations on the same theme: what a shame to let the building deteriorate so. (Not long after our visit, a nonprofit organization called Woodstock Lodge Inc. would come to the rescue, raising restoration funds.)

Irene and I walked around the building, peering into windows, imagining the kindly Burroughs rushing out with his rifle to do in another woodchuck, an animal he considered a destructive varmint. Nature lovers have sometimes been challenged in trying to reconcile this killer aspect of the man, who was known to shoot as many as a hundred woodchucks in a summer in what he called "self-defense."

David, meanwhile, took the opportunity to be annoying by writing in the guest book, "It's hard to believe the guy who wrote *Naked Lunch* came from around here."

In the afternoon, while slowly drifting down a long eddy, the moist southwest wind brought me the welcome odor of strawberries, and running ashore by a meadow, a short distance below, I was soon parting the daisies and filling my cup with the dead-ripe fruit. Berries, be they red, blue, or black, seem like a special providence to the camper-out; they are luxuries he has not counted on, and I prized these accordingly. Later in the day it threatened rain, and I drew up to shore under the shelter of some thick overhanging hemlocks, and proceeded to eat my berries and milk. . . .
"A Summer Voyage," 1879

David was reading a Burroughs essay I'd thrust upon him. Burroughs, at his most adventurous, built himself a wooden boat and spent several days floating down the Pepacton branch of the Delaware, "never before descended by a white man in a boat." I'd thought that the three of us could pile into a canoe and try the same route, though none of us knew anything about the country, even including whether or not the river was still passable. I only knew that fifteen miles of Burroughs's way now lay within the Pepacton Reservoir. In the end, the idea seemed too much effort — too much time and logistical arranging — but Burroughs's account still charmed me.

Burroughs's voyage was not in wilderness. He met young girls wading with their skirts hiked up, farmwives reluctant to part with pails of milk, cattle, railroad men on a handcar, and a number of companionable boys. He fished for trout, picked those wild strawberries, took shelter from the rain under a large and drippy elm, watched kingfishers and herons and eagles.

David found him altogether too cheerful. "Didn't he have a dark side?"

He did, in fact. Burroughs's journals are full of brooding, but he said himself, "I seem to have put all my sunshine into my books, and all my gloom into the Diaries." His intent, with readers, was not to make anyone uncomfortable, or even to ask them to think in abstract or philosophical terms. "I do not take readers to nature to give them a lesson, but to have a good time." Indeed, Burroughs was no Thoreau, and a hundred years ago far outshone him in reputation. Thoreau, with his deep thoughts and social criticism, was thought "morbid," and America's readers were much more attuned to story narratives set in peaceful, idyllic country scenes. With Burroughs, they could indulge their own nostalgia for a simpler and harmonious world.

The peak to which I refer is Slide Mountain, the highest of the Catskills . . . and probably the most inaccessible. . . . The regular way is by Big Ingin Valley where the climb is comparatively easy, and where it is often made by women. But from Woodland Valley only men may essay the ascent. . . . It was ledge upon ledge, precipice upon precipice, up which and over which we made our way slowly and with great labor, now pulling ourselves up by our hands, then cautiously finding niches for our feet and zigzagging right and left from shelf to shelf.

"The Southern Catskills," 1894

To climb Slide Mountain, Burroughs and his friends traveled some seven miles with blankets strapped to their backs and two days' grub in their pockets, and took seven hours to do so. They followed a road used by bark peelers before them, and then a line of blazed trees up the north, slide-strewn side. It was, Burroughs declared, "steep, hard climbing."

Today there are well-maintained hiking trails up Slide from both valleys, and we chose what is now the Big Indian approach, a route that would take us over 2.7 miles and 1,800 feet of elevation from parking area to the 4,180-foot summit. Our trail, the "women's way," was nothing but a walk, one foot in front of the other, over rock and hard-packed earth, as golden leaves drifted down upon us. No trail finding or scrambling was required. No doubt the other side was, before its way was set for the Sunday hiker, much more of a challenge, but I still couldn't help feeling that Burroughs made overmuch of its difficulty. By most standards the region's terrain was nothing more than old, worn, rounded-hill country. If Slide was Burroughs's idea of a high and inaccessible mountain, then no wonder Alaska had so thoroughly flummoxed him.

The last time David, Irene, and I had hiked together, it was to bush-whack our way from tidewater in Alaska's Prince William Sound to an alpine ridge with views of multiple glaciers. All the while, through dense, clawing woods, we sang out for bears, two of which we spotted on setting out. Even in Burroughs's day, the big cats, the wolves, and most of the bears were gone from the Catskills; there was little surprise and less danger to be found in the woods. Burroughs had had his most interesting wildlife encounter on Slide Mountain when, tormenting a porcupine to test the way its tail "goes with a spring like a trap," he took a few quills in his wrist.

Encounters with the Old Naturalist | 175

We had, on a weekday, the trail to ourselves. We talked about what an oddball farmer Burroughs must have been, to commit himself to such a pointless pastime as hiking up mountains. On a hike like ours, what would he have been doing? He'd have listened for birds, for sure. We listened, but I heard only the squawk of a blue jay and a few indistinguishable twitterings. We watched for animals and saw none, not even a squirrel; in fact, for days the only forest mammals we'd seen — raccoons, deer, an opossum? — had been flattened on the roadways. What else would Burroughs have done? He'd have readjusted the bedding tied to his back and the foodstuffs weighing down his pockets, perhaps anticipating the time when someone would invent a comfortable and handy backpack. He'd have looked for crooked sticks to collect for porch rails and door handles and the delight of visitors. No doubt, he'd have continually cast his writer's eye all about and kept detailed mental notes.

In Burroughs's description of Slide's summit, it had been cleared of trees to afford a view and was topped with both an observation tower and a log hut. He and his friends had patched the rude hut with boughs and made it home for a couple of nights, with a fire burning in one corner. Porcupines kept them awake with their "grunting and chattering," a little rabbit ran in and out, and rain leaked in until, one of the nights, part of the group took themselves to shelter under a rock overhang.

Our summiting, an hour and a half from our start, found us within walls of stunted balsam that blocked any view. We traversed the top to the Burroughs side and an exposed rock ledge from which we looked out on more hilly treed country not much different, but for a very few patchy clearings, from Burroughs's own description: "All was mountain and forest on every hand." The rock ledges had been carved with initials and dates, going back at least as far as 1908 and possibly — the numbers were a little obscure — 1881, Burroughs's climbing and camping era. We even found the initials J.B., which might, we knew, have belonged to any number of Jacks or Jills.

The wind, scuttling dark clouds across the sky, was cold, and we hopped down to a grassy slope below the ledge. There, we found the memorial plaque, affixed since 1923. John Burroughs, it told us, "introduced Slide Mountain to the world. He made many visits to this peak and slept several nights beneath this rock. This region is the scene of many of his essays."

I looked at the rock — that "pudden stone" or conglomerate, so well and often described by Burroughs — and I looked at the space beneath it. The man who would tuck himself there lived in an age when adventuring was still to be had in these eastern hills and forests, when "nature" lived in the cow pasture as well as beside the spring and within the hollow log.

It came to me with fresh clarity that Burroughs's value to us, then and now, had little to do with exploring or explaining wilderness, as it had little to do with preservation crusades or fired-up environmental action. His simple ambition was to share his sense of wonder about fresh strawberries, nesting birds, and the springs in porcupine tails. He taught generations of Americans — adults and children — to look closely at their surroundings and to take delight in the small things — the chickadees and the honeybees, the arches of branches, the seeds of the wild buckweed as they lay bunched in a chipmunk's hole. He was a stickler for reporting with absolute accuracy; he wanted, always, to know causes and effects and where the connections met. Before there were the words for environmental literacy, he had made that his school.

> Love sharpens the eye, the ear, the touch; it quickens the feet, it steadies the hand, it arms against the wet and the cold. What we love to do, that we do well. To know is not all; it is only half. To love is the other half.
> "The Art of Seeing Things," 1899

Love, then. Love your place, your homey place. My friends and I left the mountains, the woods, the farmlands and their fields and the stone walls where the woodchucks still burrow. I would go back to Alaska, Irene and David to their eastern cities, each of us with the images we sought, the words and concepts and contradictions we'd

Encounters with the Old Naturalist | 177

met, an enduring friendship. Irene's artist's eye had found the beauty in the landscapes; later, when she sent me prints, I'd be stunned with the color palette and compositions she captured. David's talent lay in questioning, often cynically but always provocatively, forcing me to think and justify.

In the end, what I better understood was the legitimacy of John Burroughs's small vision, the one that had not opened up to Alaska's scale. His nature wasn't bears but cows, not high-altitude peaks but wood roads, not wilderness but backyards. It's the kind of nature that gets little modern attention and is, for so many people today — despite its physical proximity — less appreciated than ever. I think of urban children who may not have seen a cow in their lives, never mind eaten berries they've picked themselves. I think of suburban and rural children who prefer to play indoors, where the electrical outlets are, instead of wading in streams and turning over rocks to see what lives beneath them. Burroughs's fundamental teaching — the importance of paying attention, finding the beauty in whatever corner or broad expanse it inhabits — is solid. What we see, hear, and touch we might love, and what we love we might care for. There isn't a place in the world that doesn't need that love.

A BIGGER WORLD

ON A VISIT TO CALIFORNIA, I took to walking the hard-packed dirt roads of old ranchland in the Santa Cruz Mountains, part of what's now preserved "open space" where the grass grows tall and the deer and coyotes roam untroubled except by one another and the more encompassing disruptions wrought by humankind. In forest parted by old logging roads, I stood small among the burned-out stumps of ancient redwoods, and on the dry hillsides I sought shade beneath the labyrinthine limbs and rattly leaves of coastal oaks.

That May I learned to walk wearing a billed cap (for sun protection) and long pants (for tick, snake, and poison oak protection — although I did not succeed in avoiding poison oak). In the damp woods I stepped around salamanders and banana slugs; on the sun-baked roads I watched for napping snakes — two of which I found to bear the feared rattles, however miniature. I kept, always, binoculars around my neck, that I might bring closer the deer that grazed like cattle over the hills, and the coyotes loping, and the red-tailed hawks wheeling and screeching through the skies. Red-winged blackbirds, shoulder patches blazing, lighted among purple thistles to spill their liquid notes.

At night, from my room in the old ranch house, I listened to the caterwauling of — yes — cats. Not feral cats — domestics gone bad — but the truly wild. Somewhere out there, not at all distant, animals of stunning ferocity and mighty lungs were mixing it up.

And then, one day, when I glanced up at the road ahead of me, I caught just the quickest glimpse of the top of a pale head, ear tips disappearing over the rise. Not a coyote, I thought. One of those cats. I jogged ahead, but the road before me was empty.

And then, another day, one of the fields was cut, the grass and the thistles laid down. I walked the road hurriedly, wanting to get past to where the grass moved with the wind, like waves on an ocean. But when I looked up, there they were, in the cut field — one close, and then another a bit farther back — a pair of bobcats, large as life, which for a bobcat is maybe a housecat times four. The nearer one was lying down, the other standing. Both were watching me in what looked to be a blasé manner, as though they were unaware of their exposure, as though they thought they were in the field that had been, hidden behind a vegetative blind.

I trained my binoculars on one and then the other, and they were huge before me, their eyes like yellow fire. Once in Alaska, I thought I'd seen a lynx — the bobcat's bigger, snowshoe-footed cousin — step off a trail ahead of me, and once I *had* seen a dead lynx brought in by a trapper, but I'd never otherwise gotten a look at any wild members of the cat family. Now the nearer bobcat stared from a whiskery, old man's face; its coat — what I could see of it, along its reclining back — was a solid reddish-brown. The other — standing, now settling onto its smooth haunches — was elegantly patterned in stripes and spots, pale against a tawny background, darker bands around the legs. If one were to design a beautiful animal, I thought, one couldn't do better than those lines, that palette, the regal look that reminded me of Phoenician statuary. I imagined the two might be a mated pair, with kittens nearby.

I stood in the road, binoculars hard against my face, and watched one and the other, and then the first again, for long, greedy minutes. They tired of me before I tired of them. The sitter rose first to wander across the cut field. Its tail, all six inches of it, twisted and whirled wildly; the underside flashed white like that of a deer, and I wondered what evolutionary advantage had been found in it. Was it for kittens to follow a mother cat to safety? The backs of the tufted ears, too, were banded with white, so conspicuous they looked like strips of reflective tape.

The cat strolled slowly, lifting its paws delicately from their wrists, paused, walked on, stopped, leapt. Like a housecat after a grasshopper, its leap was effortless, a high arc completed before the animal seemed to have even gathered itself. And, then — limp in its mouth — hung one of the gophers whose tunnels were everywhere. The cat with its prize disappeared into brush.

But the other cat was moving now. It walked around, sat, and stared ahead, and then it too was in the air, landed, and stood again, with a gopher in its mouth. It ate the gopher on the spot, leaning over it in the grass. I listened to bones crunching. When it was done, the cat stared right back out at me and licked its lips, exactly like the cartoon character Sylvester that was always trying to get Tweety Bird.

The cat turned its whiskered face and walked away, smooth as silk, as unconcerned with me as mud. At the edge of the mowed area it disappeared into the jungle of tall grass and bushes that led to the line of oaks that rose along an old fence line to the top of a hill.

I took the binoculars from my eyes and looked all around — at fields and woods, roads, grasses, sky. I was well aware that I stood not far from a landmark called Bear Gulch, and I knew, because I'd looked it up, that the bear in the name was the California grizzly that was no more. The last grizzly in the Santa Cruz Mountains was killed in 1886 after it carried off some man's three-hundred-pound pig. There used to be wolves in this country, too, and bald eagles, and some said there were still a few shy mountain lions slinking around. There used to be Native peoples here too — the Ohlone Indians — although the last of them was gone even before the last grizzly. I'd seen one of their acorn-grinding rocks nearby, with holes a foot deep from centuries of use. Bobcats, too, would be gone, had they been any larger, fiercer, or more misunderstood, had people felt them a threat to their livestock or way of life.

Just for a moment, blessed by those bobcats, I imagined what had been — that fuller, richer, perhaps even more dangerous place. It won't likely come again, despite the best human efforts to reintroduce native species, to preserve habitat. There are species that do well with us, to be sure; deer and coyotes, for example, will spread right into any available niche, will live in your suburban backyard. But bears and wolves? I think not. I think, at the top of the web, we don't want the competition.

The pair of bobcats had been like visitors — or a visitation — from a place of deeper mystery and greater possibility. As my eyes rested on the brush into which they'd disappeared, I held in my sight a bigger world. The bigness came, this time, not from optical magnification but because the world itself was truly enlarged by the presence of its creatures.

THE NATURE OF FAKERY

HANGING FROM THE WHITE WALL, with its wonderfully fierce alligator jaw reaching toward our heads and its long, bony tail whipping around behind it, the Platecarpus was everything a dinosaur lover could desire. That it was not an actual skeleton but a cast made from one hardly mattered. That it was a cast of a skeleton that belonged not to a dinosaur but to a mosasaur — a marine reptile — didn't matter that much either. Perhaps only a quibbler would notice or care about the mislabeling of mosasaur as *monosaur*, lost amid the other facts concerning the particular specimen's length (15.5 feet) and place of discovery (Kansas). The voice on my headset carried on, all about dinosaurs, drowning my thought about one lizard perhaps being as good as another, in the present case.

Next, just around the corner, I came upon a mural of Adam and Eve in the garden, leafy fronds strategically covering their nakedness. To one side, like a pet dog, stood an alert baby dinosaur that looked an awful lot like E.T. It had a slinky, belly-dragging, lizard body and a very large head with enormous pop eyes. Its pert nose and red-ruby lips were positively, creepily anthropoid.

The point of the painting was, of course, that dinosaurs lived in the Garden of Eden. We know that on the fifth day of creation, God made all the creatures of the earth and sea, including dinosaurs. We also know that, when Adam and Eve were living happily in the garden, all was love and peace in God's kingdom. *All* the dinosaurs were plant eaters, and there was no death. If I didn't already know these facts, I should know them at this point because my headset provided this history in a very authoritative voice.

My silent guide, a righteous-looking Ichabod Crane, pointed his laser light onto E.T., then onto the next dinosaur, with its lovely fake bones.

Up high again, a pair of small dinosaur models were staged as though running, one after another. These, the placard read, were dromaeosaurs, related to the better-known velociraptors. The slashing talons on their hind feet reminded me of the scary parts of *Jurassic Park*. There was something weird, though, about their pelvic areas, some extra append-ages. It took me a minute to realize I wasn't looking at representations of bones. They were the same color as the bones, but they were *saddles*, with stirrups hanging down.

The vision came to me of a naked Eve, like Lady Godiva, upon her mount. And the question: wouldn't she have needed a bridle? The narration, though, and Ichabod with his laser light, were prodding me forward to the next dinosaurs and the crashing of God's wrath, with panels of swirling darkness and a thick, gray, fiber construction meant to look like smoke billowing from a painting of a fiery volcano.

❧

In some ways, the Ozarkian town of Eureka Springs, Arkansas, makes a fitting setting for the creative creationism of the new Museum of Earth History and its dinosaurs. The community was itself founded on fakery, or at least nineteenth-century illusion.

Eureka Springs, the town, is all about the water, specifically the cool springs that bubble forth from ancient hills. It is said that Native Americans from many tribes and for many generations visited the springs for healing and relaxation. It is also said, less reliably, that the springs comprised the Fountain of Youth sought by Ponce de Leon. It is known that a Dr. Alvah Jackson in 1856 treated his son's sore eyes at the springs and claimed a "miraculous" healing. The population rush that followed is said to be second only to the California gold rush in its speed and intensity. Dr. Jackson peddled his vials of water cure, and all manner of businesses grew up to serve the sick and the seekers. The water, to be drunk or bathed in, was said to cure virtually every ailment recognized at the time, including kidney troubles, liver complaints, insomnia, dropsy, scrofula, granulated eyelids, paralysis, nervous prostration, hay fever, and "women's diseases." For a long time drinking water was hauled off and sold under the Ozarka brand.

Without a doubt, the spring water in "the town that water built" was originally clean, cool, and healthful, flowing as it did through and out of limestone layers that had been laid down as bottom-of-the-sea sediments during the Paleozoic era. It's also true that many of the sick who visited regained their health after "taking the waters" along with long walks, country food, rest and distraction at the grand hotels, and time.

The water's not the main thing anymore. Indeed the springs have long since been polluted by leaking sewage lines, and their flows have been reduced to near nothing by the erosion and runoff that prevents rainwater from soaking back into the ground. Today the municipal water supply comes from a dammed lake. The town, however, still sells healing. As the Chamber of Commerce vacation guide puts it, a visit to the area "soothes the spirit, heart and mind of all who seek an escape from the rush and tumble of present-day life . . . to rediscover the healing magic in these gently rolling hills."

Visitors of all kinds do come. They throng the shops selling walking sticks and ceramic frogs, and they stay in the gingerbread inns. At the grand hotel at the top of the town, they join ghost tours to look for long-dead victims of the charlatan doctor who once operated the building as a cancer-curing hospital. In this wedding mecca overflowing with chapels, brides pose for photos before every waterless spring. During Diversity Weekend the downtown swarms with same-sex couples searching for the perfect piece of fudge. A stop at the Carnegie library might find the cultish movie *What the Bleep Do We Know* playing to an audience intrigued with "evidence" that water molecules respond to human thoughts and feelings. Locals like to say "there is something for everyone" in Eureka Springs, and if a lot of that something seems fanciful or in contradiction to other realities — well, here we are. Perhaps the biggest attraction of all is the Christian theme park with the giant Jesus.

๊

Christ of the Ozarks, the largest (sixty-seven-feet high) Christ statue in North America, looms over Eureka Springs as the most visible expression of the New Holy Land. Other attractions at the theme park include a tram tour through the Middle East as it looked during the times of Moses and Christ (with replicas of structures like Jesus's tomb), a Bible museum (impressive numbers of ancient and foreign-language Bibles), the new Museum of Earth History (dinosaurs!), and a piece of the Berlin Wall. The centerpiece of it all is an outdoor pageant called "The Great Passion Play," about Christ's last days. The statue and the play were the grand project of Arkansas's notoriously anti-Semitic "minister of hate," Gerald L. K. Smith (dead since 1976). Christians flock from afar; more than seven million are said to have seen the play.

When you pass through the lighted gates with the angels, you know you're in Bible country. You're surrounded by devotees with U.S. flags on their shirts, and they are holding the hands of their children.

A person wanting to win the hearts and minds of children could not do better than enlist dinosaurs to his cause. That was the genius of Thomas Sharp, Museum of Earth History founder and president of the Creation Truth Foundation. The Creation Truth Foundation exists to battle the secular worldview and America's moral decline. Its seminars, publications, and videos (including "The Truth About Dinosaurs") support the "realities of Biblical Creation." (A tenet from its Web page reads, "If the God of sacred Scripture is our Creator, then He is our owner and because He is — only He can set the rules and we, His children, must obediently follow them, asking no questions.")

Sharp, who calls himself a "science educator," is upfront about his intent. On the museum's Web page, and in interviews, he has complained that the "presentation of life's origins from a purely naturalistic point of view" disregards the biblical record of earth's history, thus undermining and discrediting Scripture, beginning with Genesis and all the way through Jesus's life, death, and resurrection. "To a Christian mind-set," he says, "this is a very violent assumption." Or as he shouts on the dinosaur video I watched in the museum's gift shop, "If you've got death before Adam's sin, you've destroyed the basis of the Gospel!"

Christians, Sharp has said, lacked institutions to represent their worldview and were "only offered the state museums' approach and philosophy of dinosaurs leaving the scene 65 million years ago." Dinosaurs couldn't very well have died all those years ago if, in fact, the world was created by God in six days less than ten thousand years ago. To right this discrepancy, he created first a traveling exhibit, and then the Museum of Earth History to present the world as he knew its truth to be.

❧

Here is some of what can be learned amid the dinosaurs at the Museum of Earth History:

Dinosaurs clearly lived at the same time as humans. They are mentioned many times in the Bible — not as dinosaurs, because the word hadn't been invented yet — but as dragons, sea monsters, serpents, and creatures. Other scientific evidence includes side-by-side fossils of humans and dinosaurs and newly discovered T. Rex bones with organic cells still preserved inside.

Noah took dinosaurs on his ark. He took juvenile ones (the better to assure their health and ability to reproduce and repopulate a new world), so they would not have taken up that much room. The ark was very large, at least 450 feet long, but it may have been even larger; it was measured in cubits, which is the length of a man's forearm, and "there is some evidence that men, like animals, were larger before the Flood." Thus, the ark's dimensions could have been larger, with more room for dinosaurs.

The Flood caused the unleashing of massive amounts of energy and changed the entire geology of the earth. Thousands of feet of sediment were deposited all over. The sedimentary rock layers we see today and the fossils in them (from the animals that weren't on the ark) are thus explained. Time is not necessary for any geological processes, only conditions. "If conditions are right" — (e.g. the Flood) — "rock formation, stalactite growth, fossilization, petroleum formation, etc., can take place in a short time."

Before the Fall, all animals (including all dinosaurs) were plant eaters. Death only came through Adam's sin. Before the Fall, there was no death of (air-breathing) life — "everything was perfect, just as God created it to be."

The Ice Age was a result of the Flood. All that unleashed energy caused volcanoes and earthquakes. An abundance of water combined with a blockage of the sun's warmth (from ash in the atmosphere) produced the conditions necessary for glaciation.

The issue of dinosaur extinction "is confusing to the scientific community." However, the animals that walked off the ark after the Flood faced a very different world, and it was difficult for them to survive. Humans dispersed widely over the earth, and "scientists today believe that human pressure was the most significant factor in animal extinction, including dinosaurs."

The modern buffalo is not evolved from the giant bison but *is* the same animal, only smaller. This is because "nature is in a state of entropy, not evolution."

It's easy to make fun of the Museum of Earth History: its perversion of scientific facts, its fakery disguised as "alternative" science or breakthroughs in scientific thought. It's tempting to equate it to the hilarious Museum of Jurassic Technology in Culver City, California — a collection of curious (and fictitious) oddities labeled and narrated with great seriousness and presented as one big (knowing) joke. But there's no joke here. The displays of Bible stories mixed with dinosaur facts, pseudoscience, and outright fabrication are righteously earnest. Believe it or be damned.

There's another comparison that occurs to me, and the parallels are as eerie as Eureka Springs ghosts. A hundred years ago, in the same Victorian period that witnessed the town's peak of popularity, the naturalist John Burroughs took on "sham" nature writers who disseminated as truth a fantasy brand of nature writing. The "nature fakers," he claimed, were perverting true natural history by presenting fiction as fact. In the works of writers like William Long, virtuous birds made mud casts for broken legs and caught on their backs the little baby birds that fell from nests. Wolves killed caribou humanely by biting them in their chests to pierce their hearts. These were behaviors the writers claimed to have observed, and Long's popular books were purchased by schools to teach children "the truth of wild animal life."

Ernest Thompson Seton, another of these popular writers, went so far as to argue in his "Natural History of the Ten Commandments" that all creatures were required to obey Biblical laws. Promiscuous and polygamous animals were punished by God with pain and disease. Righteous animals, like wolves devoted to their mates, were rewarded.

More than one academic has linked the nature fakers to the Victorian discomfort with science, and specifically to the concepts of evolution. If humans were akin not to angels but to apes, what was their divine purpose? Maybe animals themselves were moral beings (thus lifting all boats in the same sea). Maybe humankind was not the creation of indifferent forces if the entire natural world was filled with evidence of goodness, dignity, and moral worth.

Imagine a U.S. president involving himself in an issue about the abilities and desires of animals. Theodore Roosevelt did exactly that in denouncing the nature fakers. He took a public position that there was a world of difference between fairy tales or fables and what was identified as natural history. He argued that we ought not to miseducate children by confusing fiction with fact.

One might think that the issue should have been clear. In fact, controversy raged through the press for five years, with Long and others defending their claims and counterattacking Roosevelt for being a hunter who killed innocent animals. In the end, a group of working naturalists got together to present a "scientific consensus" about the need for truth and accuracy. Roosevelt himself contributed a statement about the value that "real knowledge and appreciation of wild things" bring to life.

Through all this, average Americans wondered if the debate wasn't just professional jealousies and partisan politics meant to enhance or embarrass Roosevelt and his allies. Many simply did not see what all the fuss was about or care if fiction paraded as fact as long as it made a good story. In the end, the books of Long and Seton remained best sellers. Indeed, Long's were used as school textbooks as late as 1957 and one of them was later championed by another president — Ronald Reagan — as his all-time childhood favorite. Roosevelt, less popular than the fakers, was defeated in his 1912 reelection bid.

✾

The present "debate" between evolution and creationism (or its new guise as "intelligent design") has already cost us far too many trees, not to mention all the airwaves, school board and city council meetings, and courtrooms devoted to it.

To me, the whole is best summed up in about thirty seconds of a report on PBS's *NewsHour*. In it, a high school biology teacher describes trying to lead a discussion of "change over time" while a group of his students brandished Bibles and announced, "Here's our record of time." The teacher, hands thrown into the air, says, "I mean where — I have no place to go with this."

There is no debate when on the one hand you have scientific principles and understandings ("facts," if you will) and on the other a non-rational belief system. One cannot reason people out of something they didn't reason themselves into.

Sharp and his like, the activists intent on saving the world from non-Christian interpretations, are a psychological study in themselves, but I'm interested here less in them than in the pilgrims I found myself among at the theme park. Why do they — why would anyone — want to embrace patently wacky ideas that have no basis outside the agenda of an ego-driven creationist?

There are not just a few of these people; there are multitudes.

Consider this: more Americans than not believe that God created humans in their present form. A 2005 CBS News poll put the numbers at 51 percent for "God made humans just as they are," 30 percent for the evolution of humans under God's guidance, and just 15 percent for the evolution of humans without God's involvement.

A Gallup poll in 2004 had similar numbers, with 45 percent of Americans believing that God made humans in their present form at one time in the last ten thousand years. Gallup also recorded that 34 percent believe the Bible is the actual word of God, to be taken literally, word for word; 48 percent believe it's inspired by God although not to be taken literally; and 15 percent believe it's an ancient book of fables, legends, history, and moral precepts recorded by humans.

From related polling, we know that 92 percent of Americans believe in God and only 5 percent do not. Eighty-seven percent believe that Jesus was raised from the dead. Eight-five percent believe in heaven, 82 percent in miracles, 78 percent in life after death, 71 percent in the Devil, 69 percent in angels, and 48 percent in ghosts.

We're not just talking about a single concept — evolution — here. A person who believes that God created all life less than ten thousand years ago must, with any logical consistency, reject not just the foundations of biology, but also of geology, physics and astrophysics, chemistry and biochemistry, astronomy, science in general, and more than science — history, anthropology, philosophy. It's darn hard to contemplate any of earth's biological and physical systems or the ways humans have responded to them once you've rejected the basis for the origin of life. As the paleontologist Leonard Krishtalka observed, creationists would force us into "a full-scale retreat to a pre-Copernican world." (Note that, according to a National Science Foundation poll, 20 percent of today's Americans do, in fact, believe that the sun revolves around the earth.)

Science and the rest of human learning involve questioning and testing. In the creationist world, there are no mysteries and nothing that can't be explained. God made (whatever) that way; everything just *is*.

Am I belittling Christian fundamentalist views? I don't think so. They are *fundamental*; all believers need is the one book and the faith that all the answers come from it.

On his dinosaur video, Sharp ridicules the "secular scientists" who believe that ocean covered Kansas (other than during the Flood) and who can't explain an oddity of a particular dinosaur's bone structure. "Kansas doesn't have a beachfront!" he shouts, and "God messed up their explanations, and I love him for that!" His studio audience cheers.

☙

In culturally conservative Arkansas and its environs, believers in fundamentalist doctrine are well beyond a majority, and belief permeates the culture well beyond the churches. Arkansas is famous for outlawing the teaching of evolution (a law that went all the way to the U.S. Supreme Court before being overturned in the 1960s.) It is also the home, subsequently, of the Balanced Treatment for Creation-Science and Evolution-Science Act, a law mandating the teaching of creationism and rejected as unconstitutional in 1982.

At the Blue Spring Heritage Center just a few miles from Eureka Springs, a display about the history of the spring and area includes material identified as "petrified flour sacks" from the mill located at the spring before 1943. The exhibit label, pointing out "seams" visible in the rock, explains that geological changes can happen quickly; here's the proof.

The "petrified sacks," behind glass, looked to me suspiciously like concrete, possibly fired clay, possibly simply rock with a burlap texture. There was no way on earth it was petrified anything.

When I asked the owner where the petrified information came from, she told me the petrified sacks were found at the old mill site and had been put on display by a previous owner. She had never thought to have the claim verified, and no, no one had ever challenged it, as far as she knew, not in the three years her family had owned the center. When I explained a little about the natural process involved in turning organic matter to stone and said that it took a long time, she replied that a mill had been on the site a long time, since the 1840s.

⁊

What is it about the human animal that makes us want to believe, as H.L. Mencken put it, "in the palpably not true?" Wiser minds than mine have pondered this for centuries, and the reasons surely reach deeply into the roots of religion: the needs that humans have for mythologies that support their communities.

I appreciate the reasoning of the late Stephen Jay Gould, Harvard scientist and writer about evolution-related topics. In discussing the Cardiff Giant, a "petrified man" hoax of the nineteenth century, Gould puzzled over why people at the time so willingly embraced an "absurd concoction" easily debunked by experts. He puzzled in this same way over the sport of baseball — which, in fact, was not invented by a man in Cooperstown, New York, but evolved over time from earlier ball-and-bat games — and he concluded that the creation myth, whatever it is, holds remarkable power. If an entity has an explicit point of origin — a specific time and place to mark its beginning — then we can have both heroes and sacred places, which we seem to need. Evolutionary stories, in contrast, offer no particular *thing* as a symbol for reverence, worship, or patriotism — for the membership to gather around. Gould noted, "Truth and desire, fact and comfort, have no necessary, or even preferred correlation." The storied lie wins over reasoned truth.

Think of it this way: humans evolved as creatures benefiting from desire more than truth, comfort more than fact. Accepting truth was a less successful survival strategy than finding solace and community from a commonly held myth.

The world that we humans have so greatly shaped is different now than when we lived in preliterate tribal societies. Our present world is more crowded, with problems that threaten not just government and cultural stabilities but basic life-support systems. The scope of knowledge that used to be containable within one text extends now through entire libraries and computer networks. This might be a good time to ask if the willful rejection of both scientific principles and thoughtful inquiry will continue to be in our species' best interests.

I understand better what was, a hundred years ago, so frustrating to the naturalists who did battle with the nature fakers. Ordinary people didn't care about natural history truths and only wanted a good story, particularly if it was "uplifting" and supported their sense of a just world. Why *not* believe that the mother bird catches the baby bird that falls from the nest? That's certainly a more soothing story than the one that goes *splat* in a cosmos that doesn't care one whit about some random organic matter that just happened to make up the structure that was the little baby bird. Why *not* choose petrified flour sacks over a chunk of discarded concrete, and hold in that single, displayable object a good story that supports the origin of rock and life as you and your culture prefer it?

Why *not* believe that Adam and Eve got to frolic with friendly dinosaurs and that Noah made room on his ark for all the dinosaurs he could fit? Don't we love that movie *Jurassic Park*, and thrill to the idea of running with the velociraptors? How about *riding* those raptors? How about if we all believe this together and that when the next apocalypse arrives we'll be on the equivalent of the ark, saved with our friends (and leaving all others behind)?

❧

On another day in Eureka Springs, I walked through woods at the edge of town. Deer roamed the hillside, crackling dry leaves underfoot, while legions of gray squirrels rummaged for nuts through the same leafy debris. Limestone ledges jutted from the ground, and I stooped in a disturbed area to pick up a piece of orange shale impressed with a finely veined leaf fossil. The stone was cool and slippery-smooth in my fingers, a tangible gift from the earth. There is much to be said for these ancient mountains, so long ago pushed up by continental collisions, so long eroded, and for the tremendous diversity of life they support.

I followed the hollow rapping of a woodpecker until I caught sight of movement and color — the scrabbling around on the side of a syca-more, the bright red crest. The pileated woodpecker is a bird I'd not seen before coming to Arkansas, and it is a stunner. It wears its crest like a banner and leads with a formidable bill. Its appearance in the Eureka Springs woods struck me with a particular awe, since its near relative, the ivory-billed, had only recently been returned to the living from the probably extinct, in deeper Arkansas woods.

It is impossible to adequately describe a beautiful bird, and I thought of a Wendell Berry poem that resurrects the idea of beauty from the dustbin of trivial use. In "Sabbath Poem VI for 2003" Berry describes an ordinary small warbler as "a bird more beautiful than every picture of himself, / more beautiful than himself killed and preserved / by the most skilled taxidermist, more beautiful / than any human mind, so small and inexact, / could hope ever to remember."

A person need not be more than a close observer, as the early natural-ists were, to be aware of the differences among related species and to understand how slow change over time and space has fit them to their places so perfectly. It doesn't take much digging after fossils to imagine the forces of time involved in their preservation. It doesn't take much at all to notice the last leaves falling from bare branches and to appreciate how one season leads to the next, and nothing stays the same.

The woodpecker raps on the tree, and I find that as awesome as anything humans have ever proposed to believe. The wonder to me is that the woods and fields and good green earth — those places we can see and hear and touch for ourselves, and each of them a marvel in its own right — don't bring more people to the sources of what so many call "God's creation."

FROM AN OLD WORLD SEA

THE MEDITERRANEAN SEA at the southeast coast of
Spain rolls in on a late winter day in white-foamed breakers that, before they topple over themselves, shine with a
peculiar gray-green light, a translucency that reminds me of
antique bottle glass. Farther out, the darker surface pitches
into short white peaks, and then the solider sea stretches
to the long horizon: the curve of the earth, water meeting
cloud. From a seat on the sand, it is easy enough for me to
think myself back to the beginning, to the ancient shores of
Ulysses, to the Greek and Roman and Moorish civilizations
for whom this was all the ocean in the world.

Once this sea must have seemed endless and inexhaust-
ible. And then, with the discovery of a greater ocean
beyond, there must again have seemed no limits. There
were fish out beyond the straits, and whales and walrus,
always another passage and another coast, more of every-

thing. The Mediterranean people, and the rest of us, thought there could be no end.

As late as 1818 the great English poet Lord Byron, who spent much of his life traipsing along the Mediterranean coast, wrote:

Roll on, thou deep and dark blue Ocean — roll!
Ten thousand fleets sweep over thee in vain;
Man marks the earth with ruin — his control
Stops with the shore . . .

This sea is gorgeous still: the shades of blue and green, the way even on an overcast day the sand bottom shows through the shallows in patterns of golden light, all the brilliant and frilly white of breaking waves, the churn of foam, the clean, clear stretches of sloping beach. This sea, in its purity, is like air. It's like blue sky. It's a surface, a background, a space. In summer tourists flock to the Mediterranean shore in hordes to gaze upon it and bathe within it; yachts float upon it.

Which is to say that the Mediterranean, this Old World sea, absent its fair-weather tourists, is not a place of life. The surface isn't clouded with phytoplankton, doesn't boil with foraging fish. All my long afternoon I spotted no more than half a dozen gulls, each winging far overhead. The beach was unlittered; the only sea life washed in was shell from one kind of clam, polished clean, and one variety of mossy, whitened weed. There was no odor to any of it. There were no fishing boats upon the water, no casters at its edge. There were no blowing whales, diving ducks, bobbing seals. There was nothing — no thing — to show me the messiness of life, of the providing sea.

To be sure, fishermen still work the Mediterranean, catching tiny silver fish in the close web of their seines. A remnant run of tuna still enters from the Atlantic. As many as three hundred thousand people are said to make their livings directly from fishing, using all the traditional tools — seines, gillnets, lines and hooks, pots and traps — as well as, increasingly, the efficiencies of industrialized factory trawlers. But catches of most species peaked more than a decade ago, and it takes more fishing effort now to catch the same amount of fish. The mackerel in Spanish markets are most likely imported from the United Kingdom; indeed, for every pound of Mediterranean-caught fish eaten in Spain, six pounds are imported from elsewhere. At the "fishing village" of Garrucha, I found recreational yachts and sailboats clearly edging out what remained of the tired wooden fishing boats. The Spanish fishing fleet — the largest in Europe — today fishes mainly in European Union and international waters, bringing it into conflict with other nations.

The old sea is overfished, and polluted too. Half of the urban centers that line the Mediterranean — home to 150 million people — lack sewage-treatment facilities, and 80 percent of the region's wastewater enters the sea untreated. Toxic chemical compounds such as DDT and dioxins are still dumped at sea, metals and nitrates wash down rivers, and more than seven hundred thousand tons of crude oil finds its way into the Mediterranean each year. Massive tourist developments all along the coast add their discharges and contribute to erosion and habitat displacement. The critically endangered Mediterranean monk seals, after suffering from a distemper-like virus and other diseases, are down to their final few hundred, and alien species of seaweeds and crustaceans brought in ships' ballast water are squeezing out native species.

❧

I'm not, of course, the first to note that something has been lost from the Mediterranean, this most-suffering of the world's seas. Way back in 1864, in his seminal work of conservation literature, the American George Perkins Marsh analyzed the decline of ancient Mediterranean and Near Eastern civilizations in terms of watershed abuses — and warned against making similar mistakes in America.

How accurate Marsh's analysis was I can't say, but I can't help but contrast the stark scene I found on the Spanish coast to the one I know at home, in Alaska. I think of our spring herring spawn: seawater white with milt, kelp leaves coated with crunchy eggs, nets of shining fish, all the mobs of birds and sea lions and people feasting. Salmon follow, year after year, one species and stock after another, each in its time and to its place — and again, seals and whales and fishermen attend them. Plankton leaves phosphorescence in the wakes of boats, tide pools swarm with sea stars and flowering anemones, seaweeds and shells layer in windrows along the beach. Mussel beds pop and sputter, and eagles cry. Good, fecund, nostril-tingling sea smells fill the air. Even in winter — seabirds flock, lolling otters pull apart crabs, lacy pink algae ribbon the shore, the boats go out to troll for king salmon or jig for cod. So much life. Not pretty, not background for photos and play, but real, messy life — everything eating and being eaten, dependent, the whole web.

But over the horizon — ours in Alaska — new Spanish trawlers take Russian fish that intermingle with American stocks. Russia's regulation is suspect, its oversight poor, international cooperation a problem. There's concern about quotas and interceptions, about food stress exhibited by sea mammals and birds in Alaska waters, especially the Bering Sea. Overfishing, pollution brought to Arctic waters by air and water currents, the effects of global warming and ocean acidification — these all threaten the vast ocean resources that were once well beyond the known world. Today all the ocean feels as locked down as the Mediterranean — nearly a closed basin behind the Strait of Gibraltar — actually is.

᠅

Yes, once the Mediterranean — true to its name — was the middle, and beyond it lay all those other places where sailors did not in fact drop off the edges of the earth but found more and newer waters to exploit, until the last whales were chased all the way to their summer feeding grounds in the ice-crusted Arctic. Now there's no new ocean to be met and exploited, but a million fishing vessels — twice as many as in 1970 — roam the world's oceans, with fleets of giant ships from many nations chasing side-by-side the same remaining fish. According to the U.N. Food and Agriculture Organization, half of all monitored stocks are fully exploited, and another quarter are overexploited, depleted, or slowly recovering. This means that globally we have exceeded the maximum amount of marine fishing that can be supported, and that the sustainability of both catches and the ecosystems from which they come are at risk.

From an Old World Sea | 199

Meanwhile, oil and other pollutants continue to flow into marine waters. The National Research Council has calculated that at any moment in time 280,000 tons of tar balls ride the ocean. Coral reefs — home to one-third of the world's marine species — are rapidly being destroyed by pollution, fishing practices, and other human activities, with 30 percent already either dead or severely damaged, and scientists projecting that 70 percent may be lost within the next quarter century.

In *The Sea Around Us*, her 1961 masterpiece, Rachel Carson noted various ways that human activities had come to threaten the sea. "But the sea," she wrote, "though changed in a sinister way, will continue to exist; the threat is rather to life itself."

From the Spanish shore, I gaze on a pretty tourists' scene, but it looks sinister to me, both beach and sea more barren than a desert. I've heard that, in some places along the coast, sea grasses that wash ashore are removed because they're considered unsightly. Without the anchoring of grasses, beaches erode, and then developers dredge sand from offshore to rebuild the beaches, further disrupting whatever marine life might be growing.

I remember, back home in Alaska, the complaints of cruise-ship tourists — that my town smells "bad" because it smells "fishy." The passengers return to their ships for meals that come from a hidden kitchen they never see or smell, where — as far as they will know — nothing lives and dies.

※

Shall we assume that what we eat can always come from somewhere beyond the next Straits of Gibraltar — perhaps, as has been suggested, from fish farms that may one day circle us in space? Is this lifeless Mediterranean Sea the destination to which — given enough greed, carelessness, and disregard — we will drive all the world's oceans? From my seat on white sand, do I stare at the future?

We all by now know how blue our earth looks from space — all that water, three-quarters of the surface. Perhaps it's harder to remember that most of our oceans' productivity lies in the coastal regions — 90 percent of fisheries harvest takes place within two hundred miles of shore, and most of that within the nearest five miles — and that it's those same coastal areas we most abuse with our dumping and runoff and redesign. In the last century we've disproved Byron's poetic wishfulness about the extents of our damage just as surely as we've disproved the flat-earthers who thought that the sun sank with a hiss into the infinite ocean at the end of each day. There's not so much ocean out there that it can supply all we demand or suffer every mistreatment we chose to heap upon it; what we ruin no longer stops at the shore.

The question I want us to ask today is not what we can get away with, but whether we can come to a new understanding about what it means to be sustained in body and spirit, and whether we're willing to commit ourselves to life all the way around our one watery, interflowing globe.

HOPE IS THE THING IN SPRING

SPRING TRAINING IS ALL HOPE, the great baseball
writer Roger Angell wrote. So is spring itself, perhaps especially in the north. The idea of baseball in spring, in sun,
in birdsong, in hope . . . who could resist? For a fan living
in Alaska, Phoenix was only three plane rides, two time
zones, and one hemispheric tilt away.

❧

Ken and I arrived, blinking in the sunlight, after an all-
night flight. We'd never been to southern Arizona, never
faced such brilliant sky and desert-colored landscape. Pasty-
skinned and overdressed, we pushed up our sleeves and
drove off with maps in hand and windows open. Bravely
we made our way to freeways and streets and, finally, the
high stadium lights over the ballpark in Peoria.

The sleepless night, the climate change, the strange

environment—suddenly, none of it mattered. We had reached the familiar diamond, with its precise and predictable dimensions. Here, the crunch of peanut shells underfoot. There, the cry of the beer vendor. The grounds crew on the infield snaked around the hose for a last dampening of the green, green, exquisitely green grass. We settled in among fellow pilgrims in baseball jerseys, baseball caps, old blue hair and young chartreuse hair and tattoos, a nation of anticipation and good cheer. *Baseball, yes!* The game—that ridiculous game of hitting a ball with a stick—was about to be played, the same game played again and again in parks all over the country and beyond, a game that would be different from any game ever played before. Players from our "home team" (meaning, closest to Alaska, the Seattle Mariners) gathered in their dugout, catching balls tossed to them by fans clustered just above and then tossing them, autographed, back again. The effect, to my lagging northern senses, was like a snow squall, a blizzard of white blowing against itself.

And then it was time: the starting lineup announcements, the national anthem, cheering as the Mariners ran onto the field. They weren't the same Mariners I'd followed so ardently through their previous record-tying season. There had been retirements and trades and new signings, for one thing, but the starting lineup featured a number of newbies, the younger guys, the players who would show what they could do. Ah, *hope.* They hoped, and we hoped for them. That new young outfielder—I liked the way he moved.

From our upper-box seats behind home plate, Ken and I cheered, we groaned, we cheered again. We went out for hotdogs and inhaled the sweet smells of Indian fry bread and kettle corn. In a handicapped row ahead of us, an old geezer's wheelchair sported a bumper sticker: *Visualize World Series.* "Geezers and geezerettes," Angell (an old man now himself) used to call the retired folk who fill the seats at spring-training games—in Arizona and Florida both, Cactus and Grapefruit Leagues. All around us, grandparental people in pastel sun hats and crepey, sun-brutalized skin settled onto the cushions they'd brought with them and drank from water, not beer, bottles. They were polite and appreciative rather than rowdy, and the half-full park was often so still that I could hear the wing beats of doves that flew over and among us.

The game was not without excitement. The Mariners had five hits and three runs right off the bat, and the new player I had my eye on (Kenny Kelly, for the record — not to survive the first round of roster reductions) manufactured a splendid run out of a fielder's choice, a steal, a wild pitch, and a passed ball. Oakland players hit three home runs and won the game 6–5 in the tenth inning. We got to see a combined fourteen pitchers pitch, none for more than two innings, as they warmed up their off-season arms.

After the sixth inning, when most of the better-known players had left the game (stopping along the right-field line to sign autographs), the stadium began to empty. This was the usual pattern, I would learn. The oldsters needed their naps or to beat the traffic or they simply weren't as interested in the lesser talent, but their departure was a gift to the rest of us. I climbed into a fourth-row seat, made friends with new neighbors, and watched fastballs like I'd never seen before whip across the plate. The batter was supposed to see the seam on *that*?

Spring-training baseball is, I was pleased to find, the relic that it's been called, a sport out of time, pure sport, simple sport. It's not about winning, not about standings or statistics or even celebrity players, and not about high-priced tickets and giant stadiums vibrating to video screens and ear-shattering music. It's about the game as we want to remember it, in a time we might only be imagining, when what we feel is joy.

The common saying about spring training, of course, is that it doesn't mean anything. Surely the scores of the daily exhibition games don't, although, judging from protests in the stands, not every attendee seemed to understand why a struggling pitcher might be allowed to continue to give up hits. For the teams, spring training is about seeing who can do what, who reacts in what way under pressure, who can run — even if he gets tagged out attempting a steal.

The rest of us get to see the same thing — the testing, all that hope, the purity of bats striking balls, and balls smacking mitts, and balls thrown so hard and fast they have no arc to them at all.

ॐ

If spring-training baseball is not baseball as most Americans know it, my personal route to baseball was anything but orthodox. How did I get to be such a fan, people — including members of my own family — ask me. I didn't grow up with fandom, and Alaska isn't a baseball kind of place. As a child in New Hampshire, I did collect baseball cards — not because I was that interested in the players and their statistics, but because I was good at scaling the cards against the schoolyard wall and increasing my holdings. Also, I liked the gum. I was athletic — champion in sit-ups and pull-ups and the walk-run around the school that was the foundation of the presidential fitness program that was going to make us outperform the Russians — but I wasn't a team player. I spurned the neighborhood softball games for tennis.

I'm a reader, though, and one of the things I took to reading after I moved to Alaska was the *New Yorker* magazine. One of the *New Yorker* writers I came to love was Roger Angell, whose words, images, scenes, and sensibility were exact, provocative, and as pleasing as anything I could find in print. I was swept into his passion for the sport — its art, its beauty, its intricacies, the personalities he brought to life, even its politics. In those days we didn't have live television, and all I knew about baseball was what Angell wrote and the little bit of detail I gleaned from the Anchorage paper's sports page.

Season by season, sentence by sentence, Angell made the game more visible — more *real* — to me than it ever would have been if I'd been forced to rely on my own eyes. Left to myself, I might have seen a fielder catch a ball; with Angell, I watched one catch "flies in front of his belt buckle like a grocer catching a box of breakfast cereal pulled from a shelf." Vicarious though my experience was, I had to love the game.

Later, when live television came to Alaska, I began to watch the World Series. I knew almost nothing about the regular season, but I was Ms. October, buying a six-pack of beer and settling in front of the

Hope Is the Thing in Spring | 205

television, by myself, for those four or five or six, or — I hoped with all my might — seven days of ultimate baseball. Later still, when the play-offs were also carried on the networks, I extended my season.

I didn't have a team, a particular one that I followed and wished to win, or even a league I favored. I had a *game*. I cheered every outstanding play and player, every drive through a gap, diving catch, double play. I was attuned to the art of the game, however it played out, no matter who won or lost.

And then one fall, when I was lying in bed and focused intently on a game in the division series, Ken asked if I'd ever been to a major-league game. "I've never been to any game," I said. The next day we had plane tickets to Seattle and game tickets to a pennant-race contest between the Mariners and the Yankees, the eventual World Series winners. At the new Safeco stadium I was shocked at how small the field actually was, after all of television's wide angles and enlargements, and how human the players appeared, swinging the bat in the on-deck circle or standing with hips cocked in the outfield, as *not* seen on television. Human, merely the size of men, and yet, as Angell had taught me, people to envy and admire "because they get to do brilliant things under contrived but excruciatingly difficult circumstances."

In Seattle — that day and when I returned again and again — I learned that it's hard to share a stadium rocking with fifty thousand fans and not care about who wins. I became a Mariners fan, and I have my cap and my rally flag to prove it.

❧

For a week in sunny Arizona, Ken and I immersed ourselves in the season — following the Mariners as they played seven of the nine other Cactus League teams, in five different ballparks. We arrived early for batting practice, watched the Cubs' Sammy Sosa whack every third pitch over the back wall, saw Ichiro Suzuki snag outfield flies in casual behind-the-back catches. We sang the national anthem with and without local talent, and once sat behind the glittering twelve-year-old talent and her girlfriends. We ate hotdogs and more hotdogs, and

Greek gyros and mesquite burgers, and we bought cold lemonade ("just like Grandma used to make!") from the same vendor, who seemed to accompany us from park to park, all the way to Tucson, and became like an old friend.

One day we sat in the second row behind home plate, *in front of* a row of Panama-hatted scouts, who aimed their speed guns around us and compared pitch speeds and pitcher notes with one another. Ken looked up from our scorebook to impress upon me, "This is the best seat you'll ever have in your life. You'll *never* go to a game with major league players and have a better seat." Another day we sat in the front row past first base, so close to two outstanding plays that we saw the sweat fly. We reached for foul balls and watched old men scrambling after them, and we saw foul-ball catchers hand off their trophies to nearby children while everyone clapped. Yet another day we sat in awe as the Diamondbacks' Randy Johnson pitched five fast innings against his old Mariner teammates, who struggled for a single hit.

The Mariner-Diamondback game was one of two occasions we found parks jam-packed with capacity (eleven thousand-plus) crowds — a relatively new situation, we gathered, since spring training had emerged from obscurity to have a luster all its own. Other games, with fewer than three thousand attendees, felt spacious, like private parties, where every fan's shout ("You're pitching just like Grandma used to!") was audible and birdsong filled the pauses.

The announcer, one sweltering day with temperatures in the eighties, reported Seattle weather as thirty-four degrees with rain and snow. When the cheering stopped, we drank more lemonade and turned up our collars against the sun.

Always, Japanese press and camera crews tracked Ichiro, according to polls the best-recognized personage in Japan (way ahead of the emperor) and in this country a phenom perhaps only slightly less lionized. One day we also noticed a Japanese film crew; it turned out that the game they recorded for Japanese television was the first time two Japanese position players — the Mariners' Ichiro and the San Francisco Giants' Tsuyoshi Shinjo — had ever played against one another in American baseball. Twice Ichiro hit to Shinjo in center field — once for a base hit, once an easy fly — and more baseball history was made.

Every one of the seven games had its moments, its pleasures, its new nuances that showed me something I'd never seen before and enlarged baseball for me forever. But there's one play, one day, that defined the week for me, and perhaps defines spring training as well as anything.

Picture this: in the game between the Mariners and the Giants, the Mariners pitcher, Paul Abbott, steps up to the plate with two men on and one out. The obvious strategy, for a pitcher in the American League, is for him to bunt. Abbott looks, swings big, and hits a home run. The Giants crowd — aged and partisan as it might be — rises as one and applauds wildly.

The next day we read in the paper that the Mariner's manager was absent and when the coach told Abbott to bunt, he answered, "C'mon, Lou's not here and it's spring training. Let me swing." Abbott's home run was his first since his high school days.

۶

Back home in Alaska, still under snow, each morning I slid down the driveway to retrieve the morning paper, eager for the sports section, the standings, those "meaningless" spring-training games. If March is to bring spring, spring brings the beauty of baseball, and anything must be possible.

I MET A MAN WHO HAS SEEN THE IVORY-BILLED WOODPECKER, AND THIS IS WHAT HE TOLD ME

THE WOODS

The swamp forest is only a corridor between rice fields, but the ancient cypresses tower there. Winds the week before had bared the trees, laying a carpet of tupelo golds, sweetgum reds, the rusty cypress needles. It was possible to walk dry-footed among the fluted trunks and spreading knees, the wet-season watermarks waist-high on a man.

WOODPECKERS

The usual woodpeckers were all there: their bouncing flight, the sounds of rapping, scrabbling on bark. They called *keer-uck* and *querrr-querrr, pik* and *peek, yucka yucka yucka*. The downy and the hairy were there, the red-bellied, the yellow-bellied sapsucker. The pileated was there, the largest of them, the red crest, drumming like the pounding of mallets, loud. It was a birdy place: the wildness of trees in every aspect of life and death, with pecked-out cavities, with beetles, with peeling bark.

WOODPECKER!

This is the word he let out as he grabbed for his wife's arm. He knew what he was seeing, and he could not believe that he was, in fact, seeing it. If for sixty years something has been missing, it takes more than the sight of a large, utterly distinct flying bird to convince a man of what is possible.

EIGHT SECONDS

One for the bird flying toward him from deep forest. Two for the bird landing twelve feet up a cypress trunk and clinging there in profile. Three for the bird sliding around to the back of the tree, hiding itself. Two for the bird flashing back the way it came, a single, whomping wing beat, and all that white.

COLOR

The colossal male crest, of course — the brilliant flame so inescapably, unignorably red and pointedly tall. The white was more the surprise, down the neck and across the shoulders like a saddle, and the two large wedges shaped by folded wings. And the black, the black that was not charcoal, not ebony, but absolutely black, and blacker still beside white.

SOUND

He never heard the bird, not the *henk, henk* of its call, not its tooting, staccato song, not the double rap that distinguishes its tree knocking from any other woodpecker. The early naturalists described ivorybills as social and raucous, but whatever birds have survived have had to be shy and wary, as quiet as bark. They live by stealth.

WHAT HE MISSED

Not the bill, not the bill's length, which he showed me, holding his fingers apart — "three inches." Not the thickness of the bill — this time, making a fat circle of forefinger and thumb. What he forgot to notice was the pale color of the bill, the look of ivory. In the blitz of recognition, he missed that, as he missed the very yellow eye.

THE QUOTE

No puny pileated but a whacking big bird, he said, quoting Roger Tory Peterson, who witnessed the ivorybill in 1941 and called that occasion the greatest birding moment of his long birding career. Peterson kept a page for the bird in his guidebooks, hope against hope, for years after others had shifted it to the extinct category. But a decade ago, even Peterson concluded that the bird had reached its end, like the woodlands it had inhabited, and no longer existed except in memory.

AFTER

For a long time, he had to sit on a log and not say anything. He played the image of the bird over and over and over in his mind. It was too great a thing to comprehend — that he was there, and the bird was there, and he and the bird were breathing the same air. After the descriptions and illustrations by Catesby, Audubon, and Wilson; and after the photos and films from the Louisiana swamps in the 1940s; and after the late but extensive Tanner scholarship about life history and habitat; and after Peterson's passion and despair; and after the fleeting white of new video and all the talk about the "ghost bird" and the "grail bird" and the "Lord God bird"; and after his dead father's lifetime of desire and his own matching but far-fetched desire and all the desire of the world; after all that, the ivory-billed woodpecker was still more than a person could imagine. It was as beautiful and as perfect as only it itself, its living being, could be.

ENOUGH

YOU WATCH YOUR FATHER SLEEPING in his chair
by the window. The wing chair holds him as though he
is something small and fragile, something it will fold up
around as he sinks farther into it, into himself. The pink
of his scalp shines through the part in his hair, hair that
is plentiful still and a white the color of absolute absence.
Light from the window catches the spackle of his cheeks,
the silvery bristles he misses when he thinks he is shaving
but is perhaps only moving the electric razor over, or maybe
near, a portion of his face.

Your father is "reading the paper," his main activity of the
day. This involves holding up a section of the newspaper
and looking at it, then falling asleep. The paper slips to
his lap. It crumples in his hands as he grabs or squeezes
or holds onto whatever, in his dreams, he is grabbing, or

squeezing, or holding. Now, as you watch, the bunched-up paper is released and slides to the floor.

Your father's hands continue to be busy on their own, in his lap. He looks like he might be playing an instrument, his fingers moving across a keyboard. Or sewing, pushing a needle through cloth.

In his previous life, he claimed to be without musical talent, although he loved listening to classical concerts on the radio and for more than fifty years sang in his church choir. In his previous life, he did not sew. Or maybe he did sew. He was a doctor, so — yes, he must have sewn up incisions.

Now he is working his buttons. He is undoing his shirt.

❧

You have been reading, learning about plaques and tangles in a diseased brain. The plaques are clumpy and brown, like tumbleweeds that have blown in and taken root in the spaces between the neurons. The tangles are long, dark, stringy fibers, like vines; they are not in the spaces but within the neurons themselves, winding through the cells, choking. They are kudzu.

This is how you picture your father's brain: a landscape taken over by invasive weeds. This exotic and ghoulish growth is squeezing out the native order, taking over, cutting off the pathways.

❧

Your father's face is tightly set, jaw drawn in, and his eyes are focused on the carpet in front of him. He is trying very hard to think of something. He asks, "What is the name of the place where I live?"

You say, "Hillcrest Terrace." He has lived at Hillcrest, a retirement home in New Hampshire, for seven years.

A minute later he asks, "What is the name of the place where I live?"

You have adopted a way of answering these repeated questions that you hope won't hurt your father's feelings if he should realize that he has asked the same question more than once. You act as though your first answer didn't entirely answer the question, and you make your second answer more precise or somehow in recognition that your first answer wasn't sufficient.

This time you say, "Your building is called Hillcrest Terrace. The other building that you might have been thinking of is Pearl Manor. Some people you know live at Pearl Manor."

A few minutes later he asks, "What is the name of the place where I live?" This time there is a slight emphasis to the *what*, as though he knows he has already asked this question, and he is admitting that he doesn't remember the answer.

You say, "This is Hillcrest Terrace. You have a lovely apartment here. It's a very nice place, don't you think?"

"Yes, indeed," he says.

❧

Your father has lost his watch again. He complains of this each day, that he has lost all his things: his watch, his wallet, and his keys.

His wallet is, in fact, in his pocket. It wouldn't matter much if he did lose it, as you long ago removed everything important, leaving only a few dollars and a museum membership card. His keys to an outside door and a post office box are also not lost. They remain in the tray by the door where he leaves them when he comes into the apartment. He deposits them there each time he comes home unless he forgets and keeps them in his pocket or unless, when he leaves the apartment, he picks them up and then puts them back, because he can't remember if he's leaving or just returning. In that case, when he does leave and then comes back, he can't find his keys because they are already in the tray.

You look for his watch in a desk drawer in the bedroom. You look in his sock drawer. You look in a bathroom drawer and find it there.

He is delighted that you have found it. His face wears a look of amazement, that the lost thing should be found at last.

❧

According to the psychiatric social worker, there are three objectives in caring for those with Alzheimer's: safety, comfort, and moments of joy.

Joy, you decide, overstates the objective. You will settle for moments of happiness, pleasure, contentment, peace. You will settle for any one of these no matter how simple, oft-repeated, or temporary they might be.

This listing becomes, for you, a sort of mantra to guide and get you through each day: safety, comfort, moments of happiness. Safety, comfort, moments of happiness.

❧

Your mother, who is at last back home after having recovered from a compression fracture in her spine, falls and breaks her hip. Your father stands by passively, seemingly undisturbed. You, on the other hand, are horrified by the knowledge of what broken hips mean for the elderly: the traumatic surgery, the long recovery, the physical debilitation as unused muscles wither away, the possibilities of infections and blood clots. At your mother's age, you know that a majority of those who break hips do not survive, succumbing not to the fracture itself but to any one or all of those other opportunities for everything to go wrong.

But later, when your mother lies across the bed waiting for the EMTs to arrive, your father pads into the bedroom. "Where does it hurt?" he asks. He places his hands on your mother's bare thigh and presses very gently, here, and here, and here, probing with practiced hands, the gentlest and surest doctor's hands you can imagine.

❧

When you call your father, the caregiver answers and carries the phone to him. You hear her say, "It's your daughter, Nancy, in Alaska."

You say, "Hi, Dad. How are you?"

"Just fine, thank you. I'm the only one who seems to be."

You assume he's talking about your mother. She's in a nursing home down the road, healing her hip.

"Have you seen Mom today?"

"Yes, of course."

His voice is strong and sure, and you are happy to hear it. You make some more conversation, but what you really want to know he can't tell you. He doesn't know how your mother's doctor's appointment went that day or whether your sister is still there or has gone home. After a while, you ask him to let you talk to Phyllis again.

"Who?"

Phyllis has worked for him for six months. In the beginning, he spoke of her as "the woman who comes around to help people," but he has never been able to remember her name. These days he does not seem to distinguish among any of his four caregivers or to recognize them when they arrive at the door.

"Phyllis," you say again. "Phyllis is right there."

Now he hands the phone to Phyllis. You hear him say, "Talk to this girl again."

❧

You are trying to get your father to walk with a cane. You do not call it a cane. You call it a "walking stick" and point out that hikers and mountain climbers use walking sticks. He will have none of that.

You try, at least, to get him to walk with his hands free, so that he might catch himself if he falls. But he continues to shuffle around the grounds, his hands either in his pockets (when he has not remembered how to tighten his belt to hold up his trousers) or clasped behind his back.

When his hands are behind his back, you place him in your memory on ice skates on the frozen lake, gliding effortlessly across the distance, fast and fearless, shoulders back and hands resting together, just there at the top of his tailbone.

"Just like Hans Brinker," your mother would gush, every time.

❧

In your family, you don't talk about Alzheimer's disease. You have never said to your father anything about Alzheimer's disease, in any context, and he has never mentioned it, either.

Alzheimer's is your father's diagnosis; the doctor told you this only when you asked. He told you the scans showed voids in your father's brain, shrinkage, places where nothing is happening, where the neurons have been destroyed. The doctor must have told your father his diagnosis, but then — your father would not remember this.

When you go with your father to his next doctor's appointment, the doctor gives him a memory test. The doctor invites you to be in the room when he looks at the result on his computer screen and says to your father, "I'm worried about your memory."

Your father says one of the longest, most complete, clearest sentences he has spoken all day, "There's nothing wrong with my memory."

The doctor prescribes a new drug. You add it to the pills your father takes each day. After a week, he has all the side effects: more fatigue, more confusion, sleep you cannot wake him from, hallucinations. He believes he needs to get something from the basement and can't be convinced that his retirement home doesn't have a basement. He walks around looking for the basement and the thing he can't name that he must find there. He is unsteady on his feet, falls at night and can't get up. The caregiver can't lift him, and the security people at the retirement home won't help because of "liability"; they call for the EMTs.

You stop the new drug and he returns to his previous state, the one that now seems desirable.

Your father does not have a problem remembering his doctor. He doesn't know his name, but he knows he doesn't like him. He says this whenever the matters of doctors and drugs come up.

❧

You are remembering an evening a few months back, a time when your father's brain could still locate most of the words he needed. He said to you, "I want to tell you about my life."

Your father has never been a talker, and you, in fact, know very little about his life.

That evening this is what he says:

There were two teachers at his school — sisters — who were very kind to him and encouraged him in his studies. They found him the scholarship help to go to college.

Another benefactor loaned him money for medical school. When your father went to pay him back, the man would not take his money but told him to help someone else in the same way. (You know that he did this, many times over. When other doctors were buying vacation homes and sports cars, your father was supporting scholarship funds and youth organizations.)

Your mother tricked him into marrying her. He was sick with mononucleosis and she, a student nurse, nursed him back to health. Then she came to visit him when he was with the Coast Guard, and somehow the visit turned into a marriage ceremony. He is happy that she was so aggressive in pursuing him, because he was shy, and she has been the perfect wife because she has always been sociable and taken care of everything.

When he was in the Coast Guard as a medical officer he saw a lot of the North Atlantic Ocean. His ship's sister ship disappeared mysteriously, without a trace.

He has had a fortunate life, your father tells you. He has been very lucky his whole life.

⚜

You have learned that the average human brain is home to about one hundred billion neurons. These are linked to one another with about one hundred *trillion* pathways. Each neuron has appendages that branch from it, axons that carry impulses away, dendrites that receive. The point of contact between an axon and a dendrite is a tiny space called a synapse. A single neuron can have one hundred thousand synapses connecting it to other neurons.

You are mesmerized by these unimaginable numbers and the pictures that form in your mind as you try to make sense of this information. You read that a piece of the brain the size of a grain of rice contains roughly a million neurons, ten billion synapses, and twenty miles of axons.

You have also learned that memory is a system and a process — the interaction of all those neurons connecting to one another, networking around from different regions of the brain. Each act of remembering creates a brand-new memory of that memory, with the neurons processing it along similar but always different pathways. Two things (at least) result from this. Memories change with time, since they are not fixed but are always being recreated, not things but unique processes. And each act of remembering reuses some of the same networking, strengthening the particular connections and pathways that support that memory.

This explains why your father continues to remember key events and images from his childhood and early adulthood. Over the years, he's replayed these in his mind so often they've traveled lots of different routes and built multiple, sturdy connectors. These things he has told you — his gratitude to those who helped him get an education, to the perfect wife who chose him, to surviving the war when so many did not — these are the things he has thought about most often, thoughts that most securely wire him into who he is.

જ

You are driving your father to a dentist appointment. He recognizes the route and tells you where to turn, even though you have directions. You say, wanting to make him feel necessary, "I'm so glad you're with me to show me the way."

Your father says, "My father took me to this dentist."

You think, with sinking heart, *now he is really getting crazy.*

Then you realize — no, this is just another tangle. This is a blocked firing in the brain. You already know that pronouns are a problem; *he* and *she* get confused, *my* and *your.* Names get unattached. Generations get lost in the spaces. You are learning to decipher the new language.

You say, "That's right. Rob brought you here. Your son brought you here before."

જ

At the nursing home, your father wheels your mother's chair through the halls. You walk beside them, poised to grab your father if he stumbles or the chair when it veers threateningly toward another patient. Your mother introduces your father to the nurse distributing pills, to the woman who keeps asking for the way home, to her roommate's visitor. She puffs up with pride as she tugs on your father's sleeve. "This is my *husband, Dr. Lord,* from the *Elliot Hospital.*"

You leave them in a sitting room to visit by themselves. They hold hands. You wonder what they talk about, if they talk. You know your mother assures your father that she's just fine and that he's not to worry but to eat all his dinner.

When it's time to go, they cling to one another, patting each other's hands and arms. Your father bends over your mother as she stretches toward him, the cords tight in her creped throat. Eyes squeezed shut, they press their dry, closed lips together.

Your father says, "Good-bye, sweetheart."

❧

You think back a few months, when your father said, "I missed my chance."

He meant, as he elaborated for you, that he had planned to end his life when he was still able to do so, before he would become a burden to others. He and your mother had a plan. He would drive the car at high speed off the highway and into a bridge abutment.

Driving on the highway another day — you were driving, he was safely buckled in beside you — he pointed out the bridge abutment.

He said again, "I missed my chance. I wasn't brave enough."

You know from the way he said this that it is a profound regret.

When he talked this way, you tried not to react; any reaction, you thought, would only emphasize the thought, wire it more tightly. You said, "that would be very sad" and changed the subject. You pointed out what looked like a hawk, far up in the sky.

You don't know whether your father still thinks about his missed chance and his lack of bravery or whether the neurons where those thoughts were processed are now mercifully missing.

If the thought or the memory of the thought is no longer to be found, then maybe the regret is gone as well. Maybe the regret ceases to exist.

❧

When you're back in Alaska with Ken, you try to be light-hearted. "Please shoot me," you joke. You promise, "I'll build a stash of barbiturates."

You wonder if you should investigate long-term-care insurance.

At the health food store, you pick up a jar of ginkgo biloba.

❧

Your father has always enjoyed a cocktail before dinner. He no longer knows when "before dinner" is, but if you tell him that it's four o'clock and time for a drink before dinner, he will go to the kitchen and make himself a Manhattan.

Your father's drink-making is one of those well-wired tasks, or belongs at least in part to muscle memory stored in a more primitive and lasting part of the brain. He does not always remember that the ice cubes will be in the refrigerator, or where the refrigerator is, but he can usually find a glass in the cupboard and he can always locate the bottles in the lower cabinet. He pours into the jigger that is always left in the same spot on the counter, and he pours from the jigger over the ice in the glass.

You don't know if, in his current state of health and with his medications, alcohol is a good thing or not, but you would never deny him the small pleasure of his daily drink. If he no longer anticipates his cocktail hour nor remembers it afterward, he certainly enjoys each sipping moment and the warm feeling in his throat — perhaps even a feeling in his head that may heighten, for all you know, to a joyous buzz.

One evening, you find a classical pianist on the television and invite your father to watch with you while he drinks his Manhattan. You remind him that he played the English horn when he was young. Alcohol has always loosened your father's tongue, and words begin to flow from him with a greased ease. He tells you the English horn was difficult to play, and then about a group he played with in college.

You are enjoying this — hearing him talk, learning something about his life before you knew him — even if some of it is, to you, a confus-

Enough | 221

ing muddle. He doesn't have all the language or the sequencing and relationships. You prompt him with words you think he's seeking, ask the occasional question.

You are thinking that there are, in fact, some positive or at least compensatory aspects to the nightmarish disintegration of your father. The two of you are, at the moment, enjoying the piano music together. He has his drink, and you have your cranberry juice. Fresh air drifts through the open window, and tree leaves flutter just beyond. Your father is remembering a part of his life that was meaningful to him, and you are learning to understand and appreciate him more, to value the small moments.

Your father, face flushed, tells you that later one of his musician friends wrote him a letter to ask for help getting a job, and that he never answered the letter. He says this with great sadness. He says he has always regretted this. He looks at the drink swirling in his hand, and you feel his deep, disorienting disappointment in himself.

"Dad," you say, "that was a very long time ago."

You want to console him, to tell him that everyone fails his or her friends like that, that young people are naturally self-involved, not to mention busy with their own lives, and that no doubt his friend's life proceeded just fine without his help. These things may be true, but you know they would trivialize his feelings and deny the high standards to which he has always held himself.

Instead, you tell him he has ten more minutes before dinner.

⁂

"You look very handsome in this shirt," you say to your father as you straighten his collar. You have succeeded in taking away the shirt he wore the previous day before he could put it on again, and he has dressed in the clean one you laid out.

"You better think I'm not too handsome," he says.

"Why shouldn't you be too handsome?"

"The other women . . ." he fumbles after the right words.

"Oh, the other women would think you're handsome and be chasing after you, wouldn't they?"

He grins impishly. "My, yes, there are a lot of women around here to look after me."

❧

When you were twelve your father took your old dog, Dandy — also twelve, and increasingly arthritic — to the boarding kennel at the start of a family vacation. When you returned from that vacation and said, "Let's go get Dandy," your father said, gruffly and without looking at you, "Dandy's not coming back." You remember, as he walked away, the stunned look on your mother's face and your shock as you realized that he had not told even her.

It took you a very long time to understand that your father's actions were rooted not in cruelty but in both love and grief. He was not cold but fragile, and he could not help you — could not even face you — when he could barely suppress his own tortured emotions. He had truly loved that old dog, and he had made the hard decision on his own, in isolation, without allowing himself any support apart from his own upright character.

How often in your childhood you heard your father complain that human society did not treat people with the same compassion it reserved for animals. Even as a doctor — or perhaps especially as one — he puzzled over this: why we end the pain and suffering of pets, why we prolong it for the people we love.

But that is another thought entirely.

Your father dozes, collapsed into his chair, head fallen to one side. The velvety black dog with the bead eyes and the red ribbon collar, the stuffed animal your mother bought him, hangs over the arm of the adjacent chair, almost within reach, if he wanted to reach for it.

❧

Your father asks, "What time do we go to dinner?"

"Five o'clock." He has always gone to dinner at five o'clock, ever since he moved to the retirement home. Already today, he has asked you ten times what time you will go to dinner. This time you tell him, "it's four thirty now. We go in half an hour, at five o'clock."

He looks at the clock beside his chair. "This clock doesn't have the right time."

You get up and look at the clock with him. You show him the big hand and the little hand. You think you could be doing this with a five-year-old, but a five-year-old would soon learn to read the clock on his own.

After dinner, he looks at the newspaper some more. He looks at the clock. He asks you, "What time do we go to dinner?"

⁂

You are grateful that your father is as easy as he is. You have heard all the stories about people with Alzheimer's who become violent, striking their spouses and caregivers. You have heard about the paranoid ones who accuse everyone of stealing from them, who huddle in fear. You have heard of tremendous arguments, in which the confused person insists on something utterly impossible, and no explanation or substitute will suffice.

You are grateful that your father's earlier anxiety — when he worried over whatever he was supposed to do next, argued that you were taking him on a wrong road, asked again and again why he was taking pills and where they were coming from — is mostly gone now. He doesn't try to figure out his schedule, and he gets up and goes when you or the caregiver tells him it's time. He does what he's told. You are grateful that he has what seems to you a Buddhist-like acceptance of what is.

You are grateful to have caregivers who are reliable and good. They bring tomatoes from their gardens, they are attentive and kind, when they walk with your father they point out the doves on the roof.

You are grateful that there is enough money for the caregivers and the retirement home, for the nursing home for your mother, for the doctors' appointments, the prescriptions, the visits from the EMTs and the therapists. You are grateful to your parents that they planned it this way: to work hard and to save, to prepare themselves against being a burden to their children. You are grateful for the government programs — for Medicare — that pay for so much, although you wonder why, as policy, our nation spends so much for people at the ends of their lives and so little for children, education, the poor, and for protecting the air and water so essential for life. You actually know the answer to this, but you disagree with it, as policy, and you wonder what is going to happen when even more people live even longer.

❧

You are tired of doing all the talking. You have praised the weather (another beautiful day!), commented upon the news (more dead in Iraq), reported on the baseball play-off scores and the schedule for the New England Patriots, listed the neighbors you saw out in the hall, reviewed the day's schedule (visit Mom before lunch), talked about how good the breakfast melon was, mentioned the weather again (it could rain later in the week).

You are boring yourself to death.

You talk about a book you're reading, Sue Miller's *The Story of My Father*. Only you don't mention the title or that it's about Alzheimer's. You say you're reading a memoir, and you tell your father about the part where the author's father buys a house, without first inspecting it, from a man who he knows keeps eighty cats. You tell him that the father and daughter had to catch all the cats and put them in boxes to take to the man's new home, that the cat excrement was feet-thick on the floor and all the old wooden molding and paneling were cat-scratched to shreds, and that the daughter hired teenagers to clean out the house with shovels.

You father likes this story. He shakes his head, astonished that people will do such crazy things.

❧

You know that you had many happy times with your father, but you have trouble recalling specific occasions. Your father was, when you were growing up, reserved and emotionally distant. (You are reserved and emotionally distant.) He was often impatient. (You are often impatient.) He worked long hours and lived in an adult world that didn't intersect all that often with the world of your childhood.

You do remember, when you were very small, that he read to you and that you adored him for this. You climbed into his lap in his reading chair in the living room, and he read one book after the other — *Heidi, Black Beauty, Treasure Island* — from the pastel set of children's classics shelved beside the fireplace.

You remember once going shopping with him right before Christmas, to buy a leather wallet for your mother. He was never a shopper, and the crowds along Elm Street, the fevered buying, the infinite choices — all those must have been oppressive to him. The wallet was his idea, but he asked you which you liked, which you thought your mother would most like. You were honored to be with him and to be asked your opinion.

There were all those hiking trips in the White Mountains — what your family always referred to as "mountain climbing." Your father tended to be goal-oriented — reach the peak, get to the hut, close the loop — while you cast a longing eye on the polished-rock pools in the streams you rushed past and the mossy hollows inhabited by who-knew-what enticing creatures. He knew the mountains with a surgical precision: which was which, and when he had climbed each, by what routes, with whom, in what weather. Because he knew all that, you didn't need to. You could love the mountains in a more general way, and for their gifts to your imagination.

One year your family moved in with your uncle, who had Lou Gehrig's disease and needed help. Once that year, when you were doing your homework in the little room at the top of the stairs, your father came in to say good-night. He asked about what you were studying and told you not to stay up too late.

Why do you remember this? It was a nothing moment, and yet it stands out in your memory like something luminescent. You were fourteen, and your life, by circumstances that held you and your parents to a smaller-than-usual space, must have become more visible to your father. There he was in the doorway, so kind, so shyly interested in what you might be learning, so concerned that you get enough rest. It struck you then that it was *nice* of your father to assume you might study more than was good for you. It strikes you now that perhaps he thought *he* might have devoted too much to *his* studies, at the expense of something else.

$$\text{❧}$$

You are trying to think of a word. You want to describe a building that has structural problems. The engineers and building inspectors who look at such things have decided it is unsafe. It is — you can't for the life of you think of the word for what it is. It has been declared unsafe. No one is allowed to live there. It's a legal term. It is on the tip of your tongue.

Condemned. The word is *condemned.* It slips, finally, into your mind. It slips in as soon as you try not to think of it quite so hard.

How could you not think of such a simple word, a word you know and use all the time? Of course you know that word. Why couldn't you think of it?

$$\text{❧}$$

At dinner in the dining room, the waitress brings the check. It doesn't need to be paid, only signed so that the charge can be put on your father's monthly bill.

Your father looks at the front of the check, turns it over, looks at the back, turns it over again. He holds the pen in his hand and stares at the back of the check. It is always this way.

You prompt, "That's right. That's where you put your name." When he still hesitates, you tell him his name. He writes it down. Now the pen hesitates beside his name. He wants to put his apartment number, but he doesn't remember what it is. You tell him, "three, zero, eight." He repeats this and stares at the paper. "Three, zero, eight," you say again. He draws three slash lines, like this: ///. Then he writes out the number: *eight.* He has left a space between the slashes and the eight. Perhaps that is the zero, the nothing he couldn't think how to make.

"That's fine," you say. "Now you're all done."

You thank him for the lovely dinner.

In college, for one of your classes, you used the astronomy teacher's child for a study in language acquisition. You were fascinated with the construction of the child's first sentences and system of grammar, and you tried to theorize for yourself what sort of organic development was taking place in the brain, what was wired and what was learned.

You remember this as you watch your father struggle for words and to form sentences. He cannot come up with the word for television, but he tells you it's in a box. When you pull yourself away from the particulars — *your father* — you think that the process is so similar, and so similarly interesting, to what you observed in college. It is interesting, in part, because it seems to be the reverse.

This is not just your observation, a lay-person theory. There is a word for this — *retrogenesis*, "back to birth." The order of a child's acquired abilities — from smiling to speaking a few words to forming sentences and so on — has an almost precise inverse relationship with the lost abilities of someone with Alzheimer's.

Science now knows that myelin — the substance in the brain that coats the neurons and enables the transmission of nerve impulses between them — is laid down in a sequence, and that that sequence is later reversed in those with Alzheimer's. The reason children generally don't have memories before age three is that the ability to make memories belongs to the part of the brain that is last to "myelinize."

Last to myelinize, first to demyelinize.

You picture the white starchy myelin sheathes building up, thickening, serving as proper insulators. And you see them breaking down, falling away like old asbestos from pipes. Myelin is protein, and so are the nasty plaques that ball up in the Alzheimer brain.

You end up wishing that you had stuck with science in college. You wish you could understand what this is all about. You wish that someone a lot smarter than you would figure out how to keep the asbestos on the pipes and the debris swept up. You wish you didn't need to think of lousy metaphors.

❧

Your father has taken an interest in women's beach volleyball. He sits before the television, puts on his old-fashioned black-rimmed glasses that he claims he has never needed, and watches the tall, tanned women in their minimal bathing suits.

You know he is watching not the game but the women. He is fixed on the bounce of firm young breasts and curves of bellies, the points of pelvic bones. He is mesmerized by long legs and swinging blond ponytails. He has no idea of the score nor any preference for one team over the other.

The two women who have won a point jump together and slap their hands.

Your father smiles.

You smile. You are happy for the simplest of things.

❧

You wonder what your father dreams.

One morning he tells you he had a bad dream. In his dream a woman took him to an apartment, not his apartment but one similar.

He doesn't tell you what happened at the apartment, in the bad dream, and you don't want to know. You wonder if he remembers, and how he remembers, if he can't remember what he ate for breakfast five minutes ago. He may not even have had a dream.

You say, "Perhaps you got up at night and Phyllis took you back to bed." Phyllis sits in the living room all night and tells him when he gets up at two a.m. that it's not morning and he needs to lie down again. He thinks she's bossy.

"No," he says. "It was another woman."

You wish his dreams would be about beach volleyball, and that the women in their bathing suits would be kind to him.

At the retirement home, the residents gather in the activity room. Someone plays a banjo, and the residents sing along, old songs they remember from when they were young.

Your father has given up singing. He claims his voice is no good anymore.

What he does is whistle. You sit beside him and listen to the chorus of banjo and voices, words and notes of songs you've never heard but which seem to belong to this group like their own tongues. You listen to your father's whistle, and it is as melodious as a bird. You listen some more. He is harmonizing with the melody, making beautiful music.

You take your father for a drive to the area where he and your mother lived for many years, after you left for college and before they moved to the retirement home. He recognizes landmarks — the ball field, the yacht club, the boulder that marks his old driveway. He asks you to drive slowly past the house, and he points out new construction farther along the road.

You stop at the lake that he knows so well, in so many ways — from shore, from canoe, from cross-country skis and skates. He doesn't hesitate to haul himself from the car to stand in blustery wind along the wave-lapped shore. The maples in the distance, just turning orange and red, glow in the slanted light. The greens among them are the vibrant greens of the same low light, as though the color seeps like sap from the veins and fibers. You take a deep breath, full of the scent of cool water and the beginnings of decay.

You think about the beauty of the moment, and how it lives in the light and the water and the swaying of the trees, and how it also lives in the memories that adhere to the place itself, that draw up from the well the water in different light and under ice, and the trails in spring when the mayflowers push aside the carpet of dry oak leaves, and the cries of loons.

You want to say something like this to your father, but you can't find the words. Perhaps it's not a sayable thing, anyway. It's a *felt* thing, and you think your father is feeling the same thing. He is looking at the water and the colored leaves, images that are surely seated against his memories, which, if the broken networking no longer recalls the particulars, at least leave him with the general impressions of this place he still knows. It is a good place, a place of peace.

And when the particular place is lost to him, there will still be, somewhere, the leaf and the water and the distant bird gliding on its wings. They will exist in their own small moments, and they will be enough.

You say the insufficient words. You say, "The colors are really beautiful right now, aren't they?" You take your father's arm to walk along the shore.